Praise for the 2nd Edition of *Email Marketing Rules*

"Once again the best book ever written about email marketing. A massive amount of new information."

Jay Baer, President of Convince & Convert, Author of *New York Times* bestseller *Youtility*, and Coauthor of *The NOW Revolution*

"More tips—many of them far from obvious—from a master of retail email marketing. A must-read."

Don Davis, Editor in Chief of *Internet Retailer Magazine*

"Chad is one of the top thinkers in the email world! Anytime I am asked how someone can learn more about email, I reference this book."

Simms Jenkins, Founder & CEO of BrightWave and Author of *The New Inbox* and *The Truth About Email Marketing*

"Required reading for any marketer looking to build a first-class digital marketing strategy."

Kyle Lacy, Director of Global Content & Research at the Salesforce Marketing Cloud, Coauthor of *Social CRM for Dummies* and *Branding Yourself*, and Author of *Twitter Marketing for Dummies*

"Chad White simplifies the rules of the game. Those who fail to follow Chad's rules, do so at their own risk."

Loren McDonald, VP of Industry Relations at Silverpop, An IBM Company

"A roadmap to success. In an easy-to-read format, it can be used as a go-to reference on all things email marketing."

"*Email Marketing Rules* gives marketers a well-structured, easy-to-follow template for reviewing and improving their programs."

"Chock-full of practical insights that will improve the profitability of your company's email marketing."

CHAD WHITE has written thousands of posts and articles about email marketing trends and best practices—as a journalist at Condé Nast and Dow Jones & Co., and as a researcher and analyst at the Direct Marketing Association, Litmus, and the two largest email service providers in the world, Salesforce.com and Responsys.

His research and commentary have appeared in more than 100 publications, including *The New York Times*, *The Wall Street Journal*, *USA Today*, *U.S. News & World Report*, *Advertising Age*, *Adweek*, *MarketWatch*, and *SmartMoney*.

Connect with Chad at EmailMarketingRules.com and on:

twitter.com/chadswhite

linkedin.com/in/chadswhite

pinterest.com/chadswhite

EMAIL MARKETING RULES

A Step-by-Step Guide to the Best Practices that Power Email Marketing Success

Chad White

Email Marketing Rules
Copyright © 2014 by Chad White

ISBN-13: 978-1500981976
ISBN-10: 1500981974

Second Edition: September 2014
First Edition: March 2013

Printed in the United States of America

Warning and Disclaimer
Every effort has been made to make this book as complete and as accurate as possible, but no warranty or fitness is implied. The information is provided on an "as is" basis. The author shall have neither liability nor responsibility to any person or entity with respect to any loss or damages arising from the information contained in this book. The author is not a lawyer and none of the information in this book should be construed as legal advice.

Bulk Orders
Discounts are available on bulk orders of this book. For details, contact the author via LinkedIn at linkedin.com/in/chadswhite.

Contents

PART II
THE INTERCONNECTIONS

PART III
THE FUTURE

Foreword

The Currency of Modern Marketing

By Jay Baer, President of Convince & Convert,
Author of *New York Times* bestseller *Youtility*, and
Coauthor of *The NOW Revolution*

This is, quite simply, once again the best book ever
written about email marketing and I am honored
and delighted to have been asked by Chad White—
who perhaps knows more about the subject than
anyone on the planet (and most assuredly has
spent more time thinking about email than anyone
on the planet)—to again write the Foreword.

Email marketing is like driving a car. You have
to learn how to do it, but once you've done so it's
quite easy to take for granted. The litany of
technology advances created by email service
providers (ESPs) to make sending, tracking,
targeting, and automating email easier can make
you feel like you're behind the wheel of a high-
tech, luxury sports car. But successful email
marketing—like all marketing, really—isn't about
the car, it's about the driver.

Whether you're a new or casual email marketer
or a seasoned pro, you cannot take your hands off

the wheel for a second. Just because you have remarkable technological horsepower at your disposal does not mean that your email program can or should run on auto-pilot. Yet, far too many are managed (or not managed) that way every day.

For many years, the fundamental architecture of email remained constant: you send an email, people receive it and hopefully open, read, and click. But those constants are now a distant memory, wiped away by a litany of change that requires smart marketers to fundamentally shift how they use email. Email is at the heart of most brand-to-consumer communication programs, thus all big trends like smartphones, tablets, social media, and even alterations in how companies like Google handle incoming messages impacts email best practices...a lot. That's why this second edition of *Email Marketing Rules* is so important: It builds upon the foundational greatness of the first book, but also adds a massive amount of new information that provides the *why* marketers need.

In *Email Marketing Rules*, you'll find a consistent thread woven throughout that is THE key insight about email marketing success—far more so than any best practice, or design guideline, or high-tech optimization technique. It's simply this: Email is a value exchange between a company and a person, and in a world where every one of us is being overtaken by an invitation avalanche with all companies of every size and description beseeching us to like, friend, follow, watch, and click, the value provided by the company needs to steadily go up.

But even that fundamental balance is different these days, as Chad White illustrates in his discussion of *super-engagement* and *confirmed opt-in lite*—among other concepts. It seems that a subscriber is no longer just a subscriber, and even more specific segmentation is necessary to keep relevancy sufficiently high.

And relevancy is the prism through which all email marketing must pass. It's the ultimate spam filter. We've talked for many years about the importance of permission in email marketing— about how to get new addresses, whether a double opt-in is a good idea, and how to manage unsubscribes. But the reality is that permission is a bottom of the funnel behavior that falls into the same category as a Facebook like and a Twitter follow. It's simply the manifestation of something far more important...relevance.

It doesn't matter how special your offer is, or how beautiful your emails are. If your email marketing isn't truly and inherently relevant to people at a singular, personal level, you're in trouble, because relevance is the currency of modern marketing. What makes an effective Facebook post? Relevance (and resonance). What makes an effective tweet? Relevance. What makes an effective blog post? Relevance. The *What's in it for me?* calculation is being performed hundreds of times per day, across multiple channels, by every single one of your customers and prospects.

Permission is ephemeral. Opt-in isn't a lifetime Supreme Court appointment. It's a temporary agreement between you and the recipient. Your ability to successfully email a person isn't static; it ebbs and flows based on circumstantial relevancy.

Every email you send can build your brand, or chip away at your brand. This new edition provides extraordinarily thoughtful counsel about successfully navigating this dynamic.

So as you read this remarkable book, take notes. Be thinking about how you can use these principles to increase relevancy. If you can devise and manage an email program that benefits subscribers first, the downstream benefits to the company will be astounding. Because ultimately, in this bouillabaisse of modern digital marketing, the smart companies create value, not just noise.

Introduction

The Best Executions Are Powered by an Understanding of Best Practices

> *"Wondering if 'best practices' were called 'profit practices' whether we'd be more likely to follow them. Words have power."*
>
> —Mark Brownlow, Publisher of EmailMarketingReports.com

Email marketing's return on investment is significantly higher than that for paid search and way higher than the ROI of social media, direct marketing, and every other channel. That's because email marketing has a number of compelling and unique characteristics.

First, email is a one-to-one communication channel and used daily by nearly everyone, giving it unparalleled targeting capabilities and reach.

Second, consumers overwhelmingly prefer to receive commercial messages via email, because it's less intrusive and more convenient, searchable, and eco-friendly than other channels.

Third, although other channels excel at raising awareness, acquiring customers, and fostering conversations, email marketing is THE power channel for retention marketing. Consumers strongly associate email marketing with deals, product information, and service notifications, making it unrivaled at driving sales and boosting loyalty.

And fourth, email is immediate, thanks to the growing adoption of mobile devices and the fact that checking email is the No. 1 activity on smartphones—even more popular than making phone calls.

But email's impressive power obscures an unfortunate truth:

Poor practices are blunting email marketing's effectiveness and keeping its ROI from being truly awesome.

After a decade of tracking the email marketing campaigns of many of the largest retailers and B2C brands in the U.S. and extensively researching their practices, I've never been more convinced that following best practices is critical to achieving spectacular results. This book is about the practices that unlock incremental improvements in your email program, and about the combinations of practices that maximize delivery success, list growth, relevance, and other key goals that are the foundation of email marketing success.

One of the main reasons that email doesn't reach its full potential is because of chronic underinvestment. It has been branded *cheap* and *simple*, which has misled some companies into thinking that maximizing its ROI is based on minimizing its budget, that most of the money in the channel is in the low-hanging fruit.

However, as email marketing's complexity has steadily grown, more of the return has migrated higher up the sophistication ladder. Although there's still plenty of low-hanging fruit, some of the sweetest fruit can only be reached with the savvy use of best practices, advanced targeting and automation, and cross-channel integration. This is as much a manpower and know-how gap as it is a technological gap, given that the majority of the functionality offered by email service providers goes unused by most marketers.

Investments in greater email marketing sophistication often lead to even higher returns, not diminishing returns.

Despite all the talk about Big Data, analytics, and performance-based decision-making, most budget allocations are still based on gut feelings and internal politics. That's because most businesses have only a rough idea of the returns generated by each of the channels they use due to a lack of investment in measurement. Even in a channel like email, where there's above average visibility into program results, many companies don't know their ROI or the value of a subscriber.

The adoption of email marketing best practices has also been hampered by confusion about which practices are actually *best practices*—or whether best practices even exist anymore. Although email marketing is a dynamic, evolving channel—where consumer behavior changes, the protocols of inbox providers change, inbox capabilities change, email-reading devices change, email marketing capabilities change, and laws change—rest assured that quite a bit of conventional wisdom has built up over the past decade. Ignoring it is highly inefficient at best and perilous at worst.

Let's be clear: Best practices are not always determined by what the majority does, because leaders always forge the way. The exception does not disprove the rule. And while it sounds snappy, the best practice is not "the practice that is best for your business."

Best practices are those practices that generally produce the best results or minimize risk.

It's critical to recognize that the root of best practices is subscriber expectations and behaviors. That's why there's rarely any significant competitive advantage in breaking best practices. Doing so just puts you at odds with what subscribers expect.

However, every brand is different, with different circumstances and different audiences. So it should be fully expected that some companies can successfully deviate from industry accepted best practices through experimentation. Rather than being a surprise or disproving best practices, such instances only serve to illustrate why testing is itself a best practice.

If you're getting hung up on the implied absolutism or universalism of the word *best* in the term *best practice*, then feel free to call them industry accepted practices, accepted practices, or recommended practices, as some people do. Don't get bogged down in the semantics.

Instead of putting a lot of effort into searching out those rare instances where you can break best practices, focus on bringing your business needs and your brand values and voice to your execution of best practices. Ask yourself:

- Do my email practices accurately reflect my brand?
- Are my email practices in line with how I treat my customers in other channels?
- How do my email practices influence my customers' views about my brand?
- How do my subscribers respond to my email practices?

In other words, use best practices to guide you as you search for the best execution for your brand.

The on-brand execution of best practices tailored to your unique

audience is what leads to the best execution.

Most best practices allow for plenty of creativity in how they are implemented. Additionally, an ever-evolving array of techniques and tools are available to power your execution. Therefore, the opportunities to express your unique brand and show off your marketing savvy and technological smarts are numerous. This is why best practices don't lead to mediocrity or sameness.

Think of best practices like a sheet of paper: You're confined only to the degree that you have to draw on the paper—and not on the table and floor and walls. So, while following best practices separates average email marketers from poor ones, finding the best execution separates outstanding email marketers from average ones.

Best practices are particularly valuable to those who are unfamiliar with email's unique, often confusing rules.

Even though email is a fairly mature channel, email marketing experience is not common and institutional support is subpar. Marketing degree programs rarely spend much time covering email marketing, which leads to a lot of on-the-job training. Many who are new to email marketing previously worked in the catalog and direct mail space, which has very different rules than email. And the generally small size of email marketing teams may mean you don't have many—if any— coworkers to lean on.

In this environment, avoiding assumptions based on personal preferences, experiences, behaviors, and tolerances is difficult. However, taking a "focus group of one" approach often leads to the wrong conclusions.

Marketers and executives are very different from the average consumer, so your instincts may mislead you.

The chances are quite good that you have a lot less in common with your subscribers than you think. For instance, marketers are much more tech-savvy than the average person, are much more likely to own the latest smartphone, are more involved in social media, make more purchases online, and are less concerned about their privacy—to name just a few differences.

Rather than using your gut, start by following the conventional wisdom and then test to see how your audience responds to incremental changes. That said, although it's possible to test just about anything in email and nearly everything is worth testing on some level, very few things actually get tested.

Given the reality of limited time and resources, best practices provide a valuable, low risk, default starting point.

In the first part of this book, I simplify email marketing by breaking it down into two sets of easy-to-understand rules that allow you to make focused improvements to your email program. The *Fundamental Imperatives*—11 rules that are essential for all marketers to follow to the letter—separate legitimate marketers from spammers.

The *Practice Guidelines*—covering everything from measuring success and email design to targeting and testing—are much more directional than prescriptive. How these rules are executed upon will vary from company to company, and some brands will discover through testing that they can bend or even break a few of these rules and achieve better results. These rules separate great marketers from the pack.

I've included Words to Know sections throughout Part I of this book. Although I try to keep the jargon to a minimum, an email marketing vocabulary is essential for you to know so you can effectively communicate with vendors, consultants, and other email marketers.

In Part II, I explain the interconnections of rules that power key email marketing concepts like the subscriber lifecycle, permission, list growth, inbox placement, relevance, email interactions, and email frequency. Email marketing is a complex web of connections. Understanding how all the rules work together helps you make incremental improvements by knowing where to turn up the power, and how to avoid short-circuiting yourself.

And in Part III, I share my predictions about where email marketing is headed next.

In addition to the rules in Part I, over the course of the book you'll also find four overarching Power Rules, which bring a critical point of focus to the section they conclude.

Since I've covered the U.S. retail industry for so long, you'll find that *Email Marketing Rules* is geared toward retailers, who are among the heaviest users of email marketing. However, the vast majority of the rules and concepts also apply to non-retail B2C brands, B2B companies, and international businesses, both big and small.

Email Marketing Rules is a book for planners, sharers, and action-takers.

This book is designed to get you excited about the possibilities, get you thinking about your program, get you planning changes, and get you talking with your colleagues, new hires, bosses, and vendor partners.

This book is also designed to be shared with friends and colleagues. Every rule and every other centered, bold passsage is short enough to be tweeted, with enough characters left to attribute it to either *@chadswhite* or *http://rules.ws*.

When you're done reading this book, I encourage you to loan it out. But before you do that, mark up this book. You'll find plenty of white space throughout it. Use it. Jot down your ideas and questions, what you'd like to do and who you need to talk to in order to make it happen. Dog-ear the pages and underline and star the passages that are key for your email program. That way when you pass this book along, your associates will see your vision for how to crank up the power of your email program.

Ready? Let's go!

PART I

The Rules

Email marketing is a complex machine, so it's easy to get lost. The following rules zoom in on and address one component at a time, allowing you to focus your efforts on what matters.

WORDS TO KNOW

permission
Actively or passively agreeing to receive promotional email

opt-in email marketing
Sending email only to those who have given you permission to do so

opt-out email marketing
Sending email to those who have not given you permission to do so and requiring them to unsubscribe or mark your emails as spam if they don't want to receive future emails

Controlling the Assault of Non-Solicited Pornography and Marketing Act of 2003 (CAN-SPAM)
A law regulating commercial email messaging that forbids deceptive messaging, requires senders to include a working unsubscribe link and their mailing address in every email they send, and requires senders to honor opt-out requests, among other things

email list
A list of the email addresses and other records associated with your subscribers

internet service provider (ISP)
Shorthand term for providers of web-based, desktop, and mobile email inboxes that send, store, and organize messages for users and manage and block spam (e.g., Gmail, Outlook, etc.)

email service provider (ESP)
A commercial provider of email marketing services

that allows their clients to manage their email lists, send messages, track the response of message recipients, and process signups and unsubscribes, among other capabilities

spam complaint
When an email recipient hits the Report Spam or Junk button, indicating to their ISP that the email was unwanted or irrelevant and that future emails from the sender are to be blocked

sender reputation
A reflection of your trustworthiness as an email sender that is affected by spam complaint rates and other factors that internet service providers use to determine whether to deliver, junk, or block your email

owned media
Media content that's produced by a brand that's distributed to an audience the brand developed via a closed platform controlled by the brand, such as a brand's website, brochures, in-store signage, and events

leased media
Media content produced by a brand that's distributed to an audience the brand developed via a closed platform controlled by a third party, such as Facebook, Twitter, and mobile app platforms

granted media
Media content produced by a brand that's distributed to an audience the brand developed via an open platform controlled by multiple third parties, such as email and SMS

paid media
Media content produced by a brand that's distributed to an audience developed by a third party via a closed platform controlled by that third party, such as TV ads, radio ads, newspaper ads, billboards, search ads, and display ads

earned media
Media content produced by media outlets, bloggers, consumers, and other end users of a brand's products or services about that brand that's distributed via any platform, such as publicity, social sharing, word of mouth, and ratings and reviews

relevance
How valuable a subscriber thinks your emails are—which is largely determined by how many emails you send, when they arrive, their content, and how they look and function within whichever email client is being used

global filtering
When an ISP junks and blocks all email sent by a brand to any of its email users

subscriber-level filtering
When an ISP junks and blocks all email sent by a brand to one of its email users

Fundamental Imperatives

The Rules that Separate Legitimate Marketers from Spammers

"Permission Marketing...offers the consumer an opportunity to volunteer to be marketed to. By talking only to volunteers, Permission Marketing guarantees that consumers pay more attention to the marketing messages."

—Seth Godin, Author of *Permission Marketing* and many other books

For a long time, email has been caught between the opt-out marketing industry that's aligned with direct mail and the opt-in marketing industry that's aligned with mobile and social media.

Opt-out marketers have long argued for an expansive definition of permission and had a major victory in lobbying for the CAN-SPAM Act of 2003, which made it legal to send people email without getting their permission first. They had hoped the Act would perpetuate the free-wheeling, Wild West environment.

But since the passage of the Act, there has been a steady string of developments that have undermined opt-out email marketing and rendered CAN-SPAM compliance a legal obligation that provides zero protection against having your emails junked or blocked by internet service providers (ISPs)—as well as zero protection against negative word of mouth and other brand damage.

First, the marketing laws of foreign countries—in particular, those of Canada, the U.K., and the rest of Europe—stand in sharp contrast to those of the U.S. While CAN-SPAM focuses on the worst malicious and deceptive spammers, the laws elsewhere recognize that consumers also deserve protection from unwanted emails from legitimate marketers.

Although there's no chance of CAN-SPAM being revisited in the near future, U.S. marketers may find that the marketing laws of other countries apply to them because of where subscribers live or where subscribers are travelling when they check their email.

Especially for global companies, the legal risks of not practicing permission-based email marketing are rising.

Second, many of the digital marketing channels that have risen to prominence in the wake of email are opt-in, including RSS, SMS, social media, mobile apps, and push notifications. In these new channels, consumers have total control.

Marketers can't make consumers follow them on

Pinterest or push their app onto consumers' smartphones, and SMS requires an opt-in by law—with some hefty penalties already handed out to lawbreakers. Permission is fundamental to these channels and can be given and taken away at will, with no recourse for the marketer.

As a result, consumers increasingly expect to have control over the commercial messages that reach them—including emails. Many consumers now expect to not only have full permission control, but also control over the frequency at which they are emailed.

The adoption of smartphones is heightening these control expectations because consumers are now carrying their inboxes around with them everywhere they go. That's making the inbox an even more personal space.

Third, despite the advent of social networks and other messaging systems, email usage in terms of email accounts created and emails sent continues to grow. The swelling volumes have led some inbox providers to recognize that even among the email that's desired, it's not all equally important.

As a result, they've provided their users with new tools that give greater prominence to emails from the senders they care about most. The inbox has been partitioned into multiple sub-inboxes, each dedicated to a different kind of email or to messages with different priorities.

While opt-out marketers continue to struggle with the old challenge of staying out of the junk folder...

Opt-in marketers are focused on the new challenge of becoming a favorite, must-read sender.

These inbox developments make it even less likely that opt-out emails will get the attention of recipients.

And fourth, and most importantly, ISPs and spam watchdog groups have become so effective at blocking traditional, malicious spam that...

Consumers now consider spam to be any unwanted or irrelevant email—even if it's from brands they gave permission to.

It started with the Report Spam button, which inbox users liberally use to express their displeasure with senders to their inbox provider, as well as to unsubscribe without hassle. In recent years, however, ISPs have expanded their monitoring beyond spam complaints to include engagement metrics, such as opens and clicks, making endlessly email non-responsive inboxes harmful to a brand's sender reputation.

Some brands used to keep their complaint rates low by keeping lots of inactive subscribers. But now that ISPs factor in engagement, that approach has become nearly as dangerous as having a high complaint rate.

It's impossible to game the system now that ISPs require users to engage with, not just tolerate, a brand's emails.

The central reason that ISPs and lawmakers abroad have moved so aggressively to protect inboxes is that the incremental cost to send an email is nearly zero. In contrast, the costs associated with traditional channels, such as TV ads, newspaper ads, and direct mail, ensure that marketers use those channels thoughtfully.

With email, recipients and ISPs bear the vast majority of the cost of marketing messages.

Email recipients bear the cost in terms of time and attention, while ISPs bear the cost in terms of infrastructure. This difference is critical, because it exposes this channel to abuses on a scale that doesn't exist in other channels.

In the paid-owned-earned media model, email marketing has traditionally been in the owned bucket, since brands create the content and distribute it to an audience that they've developed in the form of an email list. However, just like social media is better categorized as leased media than owned media because it resides on a closed platform that's controlled by a third party, email

The 5 Types of Media

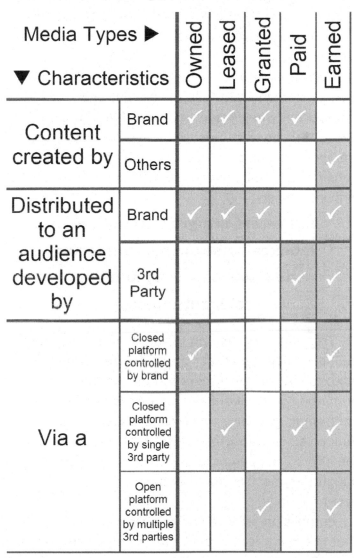

Media Types ▶ ▼ Characteristics		Owned	Leased	Granted	Paid	Earned
Content created by	Brand	✓	✓	✓	✓	
	Others					✓
Distributed to an audience developed by	Brand	✓	✓	✓		✓
	3rd Party				✓	✓
Via a	Closed platform controlled by brand	✓				✓
	Closed platform controlled by single 3rd party		✓		✓	✓
	Open platform controlled by multiple 3rd parties			✓		✓

FIGURE 1

marketing is better categorized as *granted media* than owned media because it is distributed via an open platform that's regulated and controlled by multiple third parties in the form of ISPs. (See Fig. 1 on p.21.)

This new term is needed because unlike the mail carrier who faithfully, passively, and transparently delivers everything that you give them, ISPs do not. ISPs are active players in the channel, junking and blocking email globally on behalf of all their users or specifically on behalf of individual users.

Marketers are granted access to inboxes by securing permission and maintain it by sending relevant emails.

Treating email like an ultra-cheap form of direct mail or a digital ad that you push into people's inboxes causes consumers to bad-mouth your brand on social media and to friends and to report your email as spam, which in turn causes ISPs to junk or block your email. After that happens, all the effort you spend crafting your messages is for naught, as most of the intended recipients will never see it.

Permission takes effort to obtain, which is why spammers and some legitimate brands skip this step of the relationship-building process. Even though pushing unwanted email into inboxes is the equivalent of bursting into someone's house without being invited, some marketers believe their messages are so compelling that their trespassing will be forgiven.

Permission is a pre-condition of creating relevance.

Many marketers with strong permission practices and data on past purchases, click behavior, and preferences struggle to consistently create relevant messages and remain welcome in their subscribers' inboxes. So the idea that a company without permission could collect, purchase, harvest, or steal enough information to consistently create messages relevant enough to trump the need for permission is simply arrogant and delusional. Consumer expectations are just too high and ISP vigilance too unforgiving at this point.

Time spent pursuing unethical, unwise practices is time that could have been spent using proven, successful methods.

Just because a practice is legal or there are established service companies built around that practice doesn't mean that it's ethical, wise, or likely to be profitable for you. The "satisfied customers" of such companies likely have poor visibility into the performance of their email marketing programs and just aren't accounting for the negative impact of their practices. When all the negatives such as sender reputation damage and brand damage are factored in, the return on investment from these unethical practices becomes minimal or even negative.

Your time is much better spent trying to attract new subscribers by selling them on the benefits of your program and earning their permission, which is the focus of the first 11 rules.

WORDS TO KNOW

passive or implied consent
Permission indicated when a person does not act to keep you from adding them to your email list (e.g., not unchecking a pre-checked box)

active or express consent
Permission indicated when a person explicitly acts to indicate that they want you to add them to your email list (e.g., checking an unchecked box)

unsubscribe or opt out
When a subscriber requests to be removed from your email list

unsubscribe process
How subscribers remove themselves from your email list

unsubscribe or opt-out page
Webpage that is launched when subscribers click the unsubscribe link in your emails that allows subscribers to complete the unsubscribe process

spamtrap
Whether they are long-abandoned, uncirculated, or contain a typo, these email addresses are used by ISPs and blacklisting organizations to identify spammers

inactive subscriber
A subscriber who has not opened or clicked in any of your emails in a long time; the opposite of an active or engaged subscriber

list rental
Having a message sent on your behalf to an email list owned by someone else

The Law

1

Follow the law, but recognize that doing so gives you no protection from spam complaints or other negative reactions.

In the U.S., the Controlling the Assault of Non-Solicited Pornography and Marketing Act of 2003 (CAN-SPAM) is the primary law regulating commercial email messaging, and it sets a very low bar for acceptable behavior. In fact, it sets the bar so low that legitimate email marketers should be much more concerned about getting into trouble with ISPs than with the federal government.

CAN-SPAM makes a few demands of email marketers: You must include a working unsubscribe link in every promotional email and honor opt-out requests quickly. You must include your mailing address in every email you send. And you must never use misleading or deceptive sender names, subject lines, or email copy; or attempt to conceal your identity or the fact that you're sending advertising.

Besides violating CAN-SPAM, these tactics erode subscriber trust and lead to unsubscribes, spam complaints, and negative word of mouth. Recognize that misrepresenting who the sender is or falsely using *Re:* or *Fwd:* in a subject line, for instance, is not a marketing gimmick or tactic; it is a lie—and potentially a crime.

Depending on your target audience and countries of operation, your email program may be subject to other marketing laws. Please consult an attorney to determine your risks and obligations.

Permission

2

Make sure consumers are aware that you are adding them to your email list.

If consumers are unaware that you've opted them into your email program, then they didn't give you permission. Hiding permission consents in your terms and conditions, privacy policy, or sweepstakes or contest rules is wholly insufficient. It's thoroughly established that consumers don't read privacy policies or terms and conditions. Additionally, such consent doesn't protect you from spam complaints or get you sympathy from an ISP when you ask them to stop blocking your emails.

Using a prominently positioned and clearly worded pre-checked box of adequate size can make a consumer aware that they are opting in if they take no action; however, permission is strongest when actively given—by checking a box or completing a sign-up form explicitly to receive email.

Permission

3

Never make an email opt-in mandatory for a customer interaction.

You can't force consumers to give you permission to send them promotional emails in exchange for the right to register a product, receive a receipt via email, enter a contest, or anything else. Permission granted in this fashion really isn't permission because they're only consenting to your demand to accomplish their goal.

Demanding permission in this fashion causes consumers to abandon the interaction, give you a fake email address, or unsubscribe or mark your email as spam when they receive it. Instead, use the interaction as an opportunity to sell them on the value of becoming an email subscriber.

Permission

4

Treat new subscriptions as conditional on the subscriber engaging with your emails.

For most senders, if a new subscriber hasn't opened or clicked any of your emails during their first 30 days on your list, you should stop mailing them, as this behavior indicates that the email address may be a spamtrap or otherwise poses a high risk to your sender reputation. For brands that email monthly or even less frequently, a longer trial time period would be appropriate.

At the end of this period, you might consider sending a final email asking them to click a link in the email if they'd like to continue receiving message from you. That way, on the off chance the email address does belong to a real live person and they go looking for your emails, they will have a clear way of reconfirming their subscription.

Of course, if whole segments of new subscribers are not engaging with your emails—such as those with a Gmail address or those who signed up through your mobile website—then a broader deliverability or process problem rather than an issue with the individual subscriber likely exists.

Permission

5

Make unsubscribing easy, taking no more than two clicks, and honor opt-out requests immediately.

Your unsubscribe process is competing against the one-click, never-fail Report Spam button, so it's in your best interest to make opting out as friction-free as possible to avoid spam complaints.

The unsubscribe link needs to be easy to find upon scanning your promotional emails, so small text and light gray fonts on white backgrounds should be avoided. Use white space, bold text, and other typographical elements to make the link stand out.

The unsubscribe link should never appear only in the form of graphical text or an image-based button because it will not display if images are blocked. It's best if the link text is the word *Unsubscribe* or a phrase that starts with that word, such as *Unsubscribe or Change Your Email Address* or *Unsubscribe or Update Your Email Preferences*, because consumers have been trained to look for that keyword. Avoid a generic *Click Here* for your unsubscribe link.

If a certain email that you send, such as your welcome email, is generating too many spam complaints, including an unsubscribe link at the top of the emails can often reduce complaints. If you do this, you should also include one in your footer, because subscribers are used to looking for opt-out links there.

The unsubscribe process should consist of no more than two clicks—one on the unsubscribe link in the email and one on the opt-out page. Requiring subscribers to login to access your unsubscribe page drives up spam complaints. Requiring anything besides the subscriber's email address to process an opt-out request is illegal.

While the CAN-SPAM Act stipulates that you have up to 10 business days to process opt-outs, this regulation should not be interpreted as a green light to continue to email consumers who have just unsubscribed. That window was permitted solely to provide large companies with lots of independent agents the necessary time to suppress every instance of an address from their email lists.

Even if your company fits this description, technology has improved drastically since CAN-SPAM was passed. Any legitimate email service provider (ESP) will be able to process your opt-outs as they happen.

Regardless of what's legal, consumers that continue to receive emails from you after opting out are increasingly likely to report your emails as spam, in addition to thinking less of your brand because of the annoyance.

Remember that just because a consumer wants

to stop receiving emails from you doesn't mean that they will stop buying from you or will stop interacting with you through other channels. Don't risk damaging a consumer's relationship with your brand by refusing to gracefully accept their desire to end their email relationship with your brand for the time being.

Permission

6

Accept that permission expires when a subscriber hasn't engaged with your emails in a long time.

People find new hobbies, discover new brands they prefer more, go up- or down-market because of changing finances, change jobs, and move to new cities or neighborhoods. Subscribers lose interest in your emails for a variety of reasons, some of which have nothing to do with the content of your emails or even your brand. And even though they no longer want your emails, some subscribers will just never bother to unsubscribe.

Your emails also may not reach a subscriber for technical or logistical reasons, such as your emails being junked or filtered into a folder that they never check or the subscriber abandoning their email address all-together. And, yes, sometimes subscribers die.

At a certain point, the reason doesn't matter. When a subscriber hasn't opened or clicked in a single email for a prolonged period of time, it's up to you to recognize that their silence means permission has been withdrawn.

Individual brands can determine for themselves

how long a subscriber can be inactive before they stop sending emails to them based on the impact on their sender reputation and deliverability. However, a good default is to stop mailing or at least dramatically reduce the frequency of mailings to subscribers who have been inactive for 13 months or longer, a period that takes into consideration once-a-year buying habits. And definitely do not send any mail to subscribers who have been inactive for 25 months or longer.

High-frequency senders like daily deal sites may find that they need to take action when a subscriber has been inactive for just a few months to avoid negative consequences.

Permission

7

Accept that permission grants are limited to the email address offered, even if you know one of their other addresses.

So-called email change of address (ECOA) and other services that provide a consumer's other email addresses are a violation of privacy and do not constitute permission.

Most consumers maintain multiple email addresses, using each one for different purposes. Consumers also abandon email addresses for various reasons. Using ECOA and other services to force your way into your subscribers' other inboxes because you're unhappy with the one you were granted entry to—even if you believe the address has been abandoned—is disrespectful and a violation of privacy.

Permission

8

Accept that securing an opt-in to another channel doesn't constitute permission to reach a consumer via email, too.

Knowing a customer's mailing address or phone number, or connecting with them on Facebook, LinkedIn, or other social network doesn't constitute having permission to add the customer to your email list.

Doing an email address append (e-append) or scraping an email address off a contact's profile page for mass marketing purposes is invasive and heavy-handed and is not how to build the foundation for a positive, profitable relationship. In some countries these practices are also illegal, which adds even more risk.

If you have the means to reach a customer through another channel, use that to explicitly ask the customer for permission to reach them via email as well.

Permission

9

Don't share email addresses with other brands within your company.

Just because a consumer opts in to receive emails from one of your brands doesn't mean that they're interested in getting emails from your other brands. Consumers might not be aware of your other brands and, if they are, probably aren't aware that they are part of the same parent company. To protect yourself from souring the existing brand relationship, each of your sister brands must secure its own email permission.

The good news is that you can leverage one brand relationship to expose subscribers to your other brands and get additional opt-ins. Your opt-in confirmation page, welcome email series, preference center, and promotional emails can all be used to educate subscribers about your other brands and give them the chance to opt in to their email programs.

Permission

10

Don't buy email lists or barter for email addresses.

Very few consumers knowingly give a company permission to sell their email address to other companies. So if you purchase an email list, at best you'll reach inboxes that are overrun with marketing messages and spam. But more than likely you'll reach spamtraps, abandoned email addresses, and unsuspecting and unreceptive people whose email addresses were scraped from the web and who are almost guaranteed to mark your emails as spam.

Sending email to a purchased email list is a quick and easy way to ruin your sender reputation and get you blocked by major ISPs. Reputable ESPs will fire clients found using purchased lists.

Some marketers refer to list rental as "buying a list." This unfortunate phrasing perpetuates the myth that actually buying a list of email addresses is wise and an accepted practice. It is not. List rental, on the other hand, is a fine practice, if done correctly.

Permission

11

When renting an email list, the list owner should never share the list with the renter.

If you rent a list from a company, you should supply the company with the message that you want sent. The list owner then sends that message on your behalf to their list—which you never see— using their usual name and email address, not yours. The unsubscribe link included in this email is an opt-out for the list owner only, not you. The list owner typically includes a message at the top of the email indicating that the message is from one of their partners.

This arrangement helps ensure that your message will be well received by the recipients, because the list owner would suffer unsubscribes and spam complaints if they sent a message from a partner that wasn't a good fit for their list.

List providers that are unwilling to follow this procedure should be viewed with great skepticism, as it's a sign that they either don't have permission to contact the people on their list or that the list is a poor match for your brand.

The message you send to a rented list should ideally give you the chance to convert the recipients into registered customers or into subscribers of your own. Those that opt in are now your subscribers and there's no need to rent those email addresses again, which saves you money when doing future list rentals.

The Last Word on Fundamental Imperatives

The Permission Rule

Most of the Fundamental Imperatives focus on permission, because it really is the foundation of the email marketing relationship. And in the minds of consumers, there's no clearer or more immediate marker of a spammer than violating permission.

Condensing those rules on permission gives us our first Power Rule, *The Permission Rule:*

Permission is consciously and willingly given, email address–specific, channel-specific, brand-specific, and temporary.

By taking the time to earn a consumer's permission and respecting the limits of that opt-in, you take a huge step toward fostering the trust necessary to build a profitable email relationship, as well as safeguarding your sender and brand reputation, protecting yourself from excessive spam complaints, and ensuring your deliverability remains high.

A strong focus on permission also puts you in a customer service frame of mind that's vital to achieving stellar email marketing performance—which is the subject of the remaining rules.

Practice Guidelines

The Rules that Separate Great Marketers from Good Marketers

> *"Einstein knew what was inside the box before he thought outside of it. Creativity without knowledge can be an extremely dangerous thing."*
>
> —Walter Isaacson, Author of *Jobs*

Many marketers think about their email list as something they own. Some quietly sell their list to brokers, who quietly resell that list to others. Some bankrupt companies very publicly sold their list while liquidating their assets. And a few companies have been valued largely based on the size of their list. Despite these occurrences...

Lists are owned only to the extent that someone can own a collection of nonbinding handshake agreements.

The truth is that ISPs and their users own the email channel and that marketers are granted the right to use the email channel by meeting or exceeding subscribers' expectations and those of their ISP.

Marketers set expectations during the signup process by how they attract subscribers, the information they require from subscribers, the content they say they'll send, and how frequently they say they'll send it. After permission is obtained, email marketing then becomes all about living up to the continually rising expectations of subscribers.

While permission grants marketers access to inboxes, sending relevant messaging maintains that permission.

Relevance means sending subscribers emails they routinely find valuable. Of course, relevance is in the eye of the beholder, so it's critical to listen to subscribers by monitoring how they react to the content, frequency, and design of your emails and then respond appropriately.

When you don't, many subscribers will decide your emails aren't relevant and your email frequency is too much. Those are consistently the top two reasons given by subscribers for leaving email lists, either via the unsubscribe link or the never-fail Report Spam button, depending in part on how much trust the email program has established.

**Subscribers' time is far more
valuable than the pittance it costs
to email them. Relevance has to fill
that cost-value gap.**

All marketers should feel pressure to boost the
relevance of their email programs. Leading email
marketers invest in more data analytics for
targeting and personalization, more automation for
messaging, and more design and coding resources
to increase the functionality and user-friendliness
of their emails. These leaders are causing the
expectations of all email users to increase.

At the same time, ISPs and other tool providers
are adding functionality to help email users
separate important email from the other messages
received—whether it's flagging emails from their
contacts or filtering marketing messages into a
special folder.

**Staying out of the junk folder
was the past decade's challenge.
Being a must-read sender
is this decade's.**

Relevance is the key to succeeding in this new
environment and creating relevance is a major focus
of the remaining rules, which cover everything from
measuring program success and building a
productive list to email design and testing.

These Practice Guidelines are not an absolute answer to what you should do, but rather provide strong directional guidance. You have to find the best execution for your organization within these guidelines.

Program Success

"Data-driven marketing is the engine behind improved marketing results, and it creates measurable internal accountability as marketers become more effective in planning, executing, and proving the value of their work."

—Lisa Arthur, Author of *Big Data Marketing*

Most CEOs could care less about what your open and click rates are. While such metrics are important secondary indicators of program health, CEOs want to know how the email program is helping the business succeed. For most brands, success is quantifiable in terms of the revenue and profits generated by the email program, email average order size, subscriber lifetime value, and other financial-focused metrics.

WORDS TO KNOW

email metrics
Measurements of the effectiveness of your email marketing program

open
When the images in an email are loaded or rendered, which typically happens when a subscriber views an email with images enabled

click
When a subscriber selects a link or linked image in an email with a mouse, trackpad, tap of a touchscreen, etc. and visits the associated webpage

engagement
Opens, clicks, and other positive indications that a subscriber is finding value in receiving emails from a brand

conversion
When a subscriber clicks through an email and then makes a purchase, registers for an event, or takes another action requested by the email

subscriber lifetime value
The cumulative profit generated by a subscriber during their time on your list

email client or reader
An application or web interface that displays emails and allows users to reply, forward, and interact with the content of the message

Program Success

12

Focus on maximizing the value of a subscriber, not on maximizing the results of a campaign.

Every company faces pressure to maximize short-term results; however, the ultimate goal of every business should be to maximize long-term results. In email marketing, that means looking at the lifetime value of a subscriber rather than per-campaign results, which can be deceptive since some campaigns work indirectly by boosting the effectiveness of future campaigns.

Although you can use a variety of techniques and the mechanics vary depending on the software available to you, the simplest way to calculate subscriber lifetime value is to multiply the average monthly profit per subscriber by the average retention time of a subscriber in months.

This holistic, subscriber-centric approach looks at the cumulative effect of your email marketing efforts on your subscribers. And although this view focuses on profits, it also recognizes that campaigns and content that keep subscribers engaged and primed to convert in the future are also valuable.

This approach also acknowledges that tactics,

content, gimmicks, and tricks that diminish trust, lower engagement, or increase unsubscribes and spam complaints are to be minimized because they diminish lifetime value.

In addition to lifetime value—or as a crude alternative to it—you might consider looking at your subscribers' behavior over a period of time by using open reach, click reach, and conversion reach metrics. For instance, measuring your click reach over the past quarter would mean measuring the percentage of your subscribers who clicked at least once during that time.

The key is to avoid a campaign-by-campaign mentality when looking at data, because that can cause you to misunderstand how subscribers are reacting to your overall messaging and unintentionally make campaign-specific decisions that reduce the overall effectiveness of your email program.

Program Success

13

Measure your negative performance metrics, not just your positive ones.

When evaluating strategies and tactics, make sure you're seeing the whole picture by measuring negative metrics such as unsubscribes and spam complaints—and perhaps even negative social media chatter, word of mouth, and other indications of brand impression.

Ignoring negative indicators is tempting, especially when positive indicators are high, but negative ones should be minimized because they diminish the success of your future campaigns by reducing engagement or decreasing the size of your list.

Program Success

14

View email performance by subscriber segments, paying close attention to how your most valuable subscribers react.

Looking at the performance of a campaign or series of campaigns on your entire subscriber base can conceal important trends. In particular, it can conceal how your campaigns are affecting your most valuable subscribers.

The majority of your email marketing revenue will be generated by a minority of your subscribers— perhaps a very small minority. So pay extra attention to how your campaigns affect these subscribers, especially in terms of complaints and unsubscribes.

If you find some of your campaigns work best on certain groups of subscribers, then in the future, those campaigns can be sent to just the groups that reacted positively.

Program Success

15

Recognize that many of the actions prompted by emails are not easily trackable or measurable.

Although more quantifiable than most other channels, email is not nearly as measureable as it's often portrayed because subscribers often respond to emails in ways that are untrackable or very difficult to track. Depending on your audience and business model, more than 50% of your email response might not be readily apparent.

For instance, some subscribers will type in the URL of your site into their browser or search for your brand on a social media site rather than clicking though one of your emails. Others will visit your store or event offline after seeing it promoted in an email. Some use one email address to subscribe to promotional emails and another account when making purchases. Still others will forward an email to their spouse or to friends, who will take action. And then there's word of mouth and social sharing.

Using promo codes that are unique to a particular subscriber and promoting printable and mobile coupons—particularly if those are also trackable back to individual subscribers—are a couple of ways to help measure the pass-along and offline influence of email.

Another, even better, way is to do a withhold study, where you do not send promotional emails to a group of subscribers for a while (often a month) and then compare their activity across all channels to subscribers who received emails. This approach provides insights into the incremental sales attributable solely to email while filtering out sales that would have happened anyway without email's influence.

While you clearly forego revenue from the group you withheld emails from, the results of these studies can provide powerful evidence of email's impact on your customers, evidence that you can use to make a business case for more investments and to get stronger buy-in from other groups within your business.

Program Success

16

Don't attach too much meaning
to your open rates.

The open rate is really a misnomer, because it doesn't accurately reflect the percent of recipients that viewed the contents of your email. An open is registered only if a recipient views an email with images enabled so that an invisible tracking pixel is rendered. For that reason, even if a recipient reads an email top to bottom, no open is recorded if images are blocked. Blocking images is fairly common, which makes open rates misleading.

On the other hand, just because an open was recorded doesn't mean that the recipient gave the email much or any consideration. They could have just been flipping through their emails and the images in your email loaded just for a split second before they continued on to the next email. Moreover, some email clients automatically download images, generating false opens.

More importantly, opens are of marginal use as a success metric because generating opens is rarely the primary goal of a campaign and lots of opens doesn't necessarily translate into lots of sales. In fact, maximizing your open rate on individual campaigns can actually lead to fewer clicks and lower conversions, because the tactics that increase opens—such as short, vague subject lines—often suppress the response to the email's message.

Therefore, although opens are worth tracking—as the trends, spikes, and dips can contribute to the overall picture of program health—look further down the email funnel for truly meaningful activity.

Program Success

17

Benchmark yourself primarily against yourself.

Everyone wants to know how their email program stacks up against others, but external benchmarks are of little use for a number of reasons.

First, most aggregations of data are not going to be relevant to your industry or company. Even if the benchmark is for your industry, accounting for differences between companies of different sizes that operate within different sub-verticals is impossible.

Second, the open rate and click rate data that is typically shared may not be very useful. Because brands manage their lists differently, these numbers don't provide an apples-to-apples comparison.

And third, beating an external benchmark can give you a false sense of security and make you complacent when you shouldn't be.

All of that said, if you are massively trailing external benchmarks, changes might be needed. Otherwise, focus on systematically beating your own performance.

Deliverability

"If your reputation sucks, none of it matters. People with lousy products, crummy business practices, and shady backgrounds get found out. And word spreads with frightening speed."

—Sonia Simone, Chief Marketing Officer of Copyblogger

Your sender reputation and the percentage of your emails that make it to your subscribers' inboxes are heavily influenced by your permission practices, but your signup processes, complaint rate, and other factors also play a role.

WORDS TO KNOW

deliverability
All of the issues involved with getting commercial emails delivered to their intended recipients' inboxes

delivered
When email makes it to the intended recipient's inbox or junk folder, as opposed to being blocked

inbox placement rate
The percentage of emails sent by a brand or from an IP address that reaches their intended recipients' inboxes, as opposed to being blocked or junked

bounced
When email is rejected by an internet service provider because it was sent to an unknown email address (hard bounce) or because of a temporary condition like the recipient's mailbox being full (soft bounce)

feedback loop (FBL)
A mechanism through which ISPs and other inbox providers notify email senders of spam complaints by their subscribers, allowing senders to unsubscribe those subscribers

shared IP address
An IP address from which multiple companies send email, with all of them contributing to the sender reputation of that address

dedicated IP address
An IP address from which only one company sends email, making that company solely responsible for the sender reputation of that address

throttling
When an internet service provider slows the rate at which they deliver a sender's emails to their users

junked or bulked
When emails are routed to a recipient's junk or spam folder by an ISP

blocked
When an ISP prevents your emails from being delivered to their users

blacklist
A list of senders of spam typically maintained by an independent organization that is used by ISPs to determine whether and where to deliver email

email authentication
A variety of methods that help ISPs accurately identify email sent by a brand, including Domain Keys Identified Mail (DKIM), Sender Policy Framework (SPF), and Domain-based Message Authentication, Reporting & Conformance (DMARC)

freemail
An email account that is available for free from Yahoo, AOL, Gmail, Outlook.com, or another ISP

content filtering
When an ISP evaluates an email's subject line and other content as part of its process to decide whether and where the mail should be delivered

role-based email address
An email address that begins with webmaster@, sales@, info@, press@, or a similar function-based descriptor denoting that messages sent to this

address are likely seen by or forwarded to more than one person

list hygiene
Ensuring that your email list is free of invalid and undeliverable email addresses, role-based email addresses, spam traps, unconfirmed email addresses, and chronically inactive subscribers

confirmed or double opt-in
The process of sending a subscription activation or opt-in confirmation email to a new subscriber that requires them to click a link in that email to confirm their signup or else receive no additional emails

double entry confirmation
Requiring a would-be subscriber to enter their email address again in a *confirm email address* field on a subscription form and requiring that the two entries match in order to reduce entry errors

Deliverability

18

Use an email service provider to send your commercial email.

The technical issues around sending commercial email are now complicated enough that using anything less than a professional-grade service is very risky and using homegrown software is unwise for all but the most sophisticated companies.

In addition to providing analytics, targeting, testing, and other functionality, email service providers (ESPs) handle many issues that affect your deliverability. For example, ESPs remove email addresses that hard bounce, monitor feedback loops and remove complainers, set up servers properly, send emails at a rate that's acceptable to each ISP, and help you determine whether a shared or dedicated IP address is best.

Thankfully, no matter how small or large your email needs are or what industry you're in, many ESPs are available.

Deliverability

19

Accept that ESPs have relatively little control over the deliverability of your emails.

Although using an ESP certainly helps your deliverability, the most critical factor affecting whether your emails reach your subscribers' inboxes is your sender reputation, which is a direct consequence of your permission practices, expectation setting, email frequency, how relevant your subscribers think your emails are, and how you handle subscribers who are no longer engaging with your emails.

Those factors determine whether your sends generate too many bounces from bad email addresses, too many spam complaints, and too little engagement in terms of opens and clicks, causing ISPs to throttle, junk, or block your emails.

Deliverability

20

Use email authentication and send from a domain you control.

Email authentication involves a variety of methods that help ISPs accurately identify email sent by a brand. Authenticating your emails increases your deliverability, protects your sender reputation, and makes it easier for ISPs to identify when your brand is being spoofed by spammers and phishers.

Authentication methods include Domain Keys Identified Mail (DKIM), Sender Policy Framework (SPF), and Domain-based Message Authentication, Reporting & Conformance (DMARC). As with so many things in the email world, there are no universal standards around authentication, so you'll likely need to use two or more methods. Your ESP or a consultant can help you determine your needs and authenticate your email.

Because of developments around DMARC, do not use a Yahoo, AOL, Gmail, Hotmail, or other freemail address as your *from* address because your emails will be blocked at many ISPs. Instead, send emails from a domain that you control, which makes for a stronger brand impression anyway.

Deliverability

21

Keep your spam complaint rate under 0.1%, preferably well under.

Consult with your email service provider (ESP) for their recommendations and understand your contractual obligations to them, but in general keeping your complaint rate under 1 for every 1,000 emails you send will keep you in the good graces of both ISPs and your ESP. Your ESP will report your complaint rate to you based on the feedback loops of ISPs.

Exceeding that 0.1% limit puts you at risk of having your emails junked or blocked by ISPs and of being sanctioned or terminated as a client by your ESP.

Although that's the recommended limit, be aware that most brands are able to maintain a complaint rate of less than 0.05%, so it would be wise to aim to be in the company of the majority. If the standard does change, it's more likely to get tighter rather than looser.

Deliverability

22

Don't obsess over content filtering when writing subject lines and creating email content.

Although it used to be a concern, nowadays your subject lines and the words and images in your emails are given relatively little weight when ISPs determine whether to deliver your emails. Using exclamation marks, all caps, and words such as *free* and *offer* in your subject lines will not affect your deliverability unless you have other factors that cause ISPs to view your emails as spam.

Although your words might not be that important, the links that you use in your emails are. ISPs pay attention to the sites you're linking to and take note if you use shortened URLs, which are routinely used by spammers to conceal the destination of a link. So only link to reputable sites and avoid URL shorteners.

Corporate email filters might give more weight to subject lines and email content, so business-to-business email marketers face some additional uncertainties that business-to-consumer email marketers don't have to worry about as much. Content scoring tools exist that can help you identify some potential problems.

Deliverability

23

Avoid overreacting to the introduction of new inbox organization tools and services.

The inbox is a dynamic place. Not only do ISPs and other inbox providers release new functionality on a regular basis, but third parties also create add-ons and services that affect inboxes. Although some of these developments are worth your time and consideration, those aimed at helping email users better organize and sort the emails they receive are not.

Historically, announcements of these kinds of tools have created the greatest buzz, the most handwringing, and the biggest distractions. The fear is always that marketers' emails will get less attention or, worse, exiled to a place that email users never check.

However, these developments generally benefit email marketers by making inboxes a more pleasant and efficient place for consumers to visit and spend time. What has happened consistently is that marketers who send at least modestly relevant emails are rewarded with increases in engagement by these tools, while marketers sending emails that are poorly received by subscribers see their engagement fall further.

For those marketers who are concerned that they'll be negatively impacted by these developments, the best protection is to focus on sending relevant emails. Trying to fight or game these tools is a losing strategy, as the trend toward users having more control of their inboxes is only gaining momentum.

Deliverability

24

Don't add role-based email addresses to your email list.

Role-based email addresses are those that begin with function-based descriptors such as *info@*, *webmaster@*, *sales@*, and *press@*. These addresses are a serious risk to your deliverability for a couple of reasons.

First, emails sent to these addresses are very likely seen by or forwarded to multiple people, all of whom might not be as interested in receiving your messages as the one person who opted in. Because of that, messages sent to these addresses are more likely to generate spam complaints.

And second, these addresses tend to be published publicly on websites, which means they are scraped, harvested, and collected by spammers, who send the addresses a lot of spam and sell the addresses to others. ISPs are aware of this, so having role-based addresses on your email list may be seen as a sign that you are harvesting email addresses or buying lists. Either gets you labeled a spammer and gets your emails blocked.

Reject these addresses at the time of signup, asking people to use their personal email address instead.

Deliverability

25

Use confirmed opt-in to protect yourself from low-quality email acquisition sources.

When using email acquisition sources that are outside of your organization such as list rentals or sources that have proven to produce low-quality subscribers for you, using a confirmed opt-in (COI) process can protect your list quality from slipping.

This involves sending a subscription activation or opt-in confirmation email to a new subscriber that requires them to click to confirm their signup. If they don't confirm, then they receive no additional emails. This ensures that you're adding active email addresses and subscribers who have a genuine interest in receiving your emails.

COI can also protect you from poor email acquisition processes. For instance, although call center email signups generate quality subscribers, recording email addresses can be prone to errors because of verbal transcription errors. In-store signup can be equally troublesome because of misread handwriting.

Sometimes these errors can lead to spamtraps getting onto your list. Because ISPs and blacklisting organizations such as Spamhaus use these email addresses to identify spammers, having even one spamtrap on your list can seriously affect your deliverability.

Process improvements—such as having subscribers enter their email addresses in a second field as part of a double entry confirmation, having them enter it themselves using a tablet or pinpad, and allowing store customers to visually verify that the store associate collected their address accurately—can help resolve these issues. Tools that identify common misspellings, such as *someone@hotmali.com* or *someone@aol.ocm*, can also help. However, COI is an ironclad method for addressing these kinds of quality issues, although it will significantly slow list growth from sources where it's used.

Confirmed opt-in might also be desirable when you want proof that the address owner signed up, which might be necessary in certain cases such as when minors are involved.

And finally, as mentioned earlier, laws in some countries may require COI in all instances. If you operate in other countries besides the U.S., please consult an attorney to determine your risks and obligations.

List Building & Profiling

"Customer loyalty is mostly about
choosing the right customers."
—John Jantsch, Author of *Duct Tape Marketing*

Locating the best sources of quality subscribers
and creating a subscription process that's as
friction-free as possible are key to building a
productive, low-risk email list. Determining what
information to ask for, when to ask for it, and how
to ask for it are important considerations when
trying to maximize form completions, either during
acquisition or later in the email relationship.

WORDS TO KNOW

list building or acquisition
The process of adding email addresses to your mailing list

email acquisition source
The form or mechanism through which a subscriber opts in, or the ad, sign, or other vehicle that causes them to opt in

opt-in confirmation page
Webpage or app messaging that follows a successful email signup

mailstream
The emails resulting from a single opt-in or preference selection

social sign-in
Using the login information from a social network to sign in to a third-party website

preference center
Webpage that displays a subscriber's email address and other details, such as profile information (zip code, etc.) and communication preferences (topics of interest, etc.), and allows them to make changes as well as unsubscribe

progressive profiling
Collecting additional demographic data and information about interests from subscribers by periodically asking them questions via email

List Building & Profiling

26

Recognize that not all subscribers are equally valuable or desirable.

The expectations of your subscribers—and therefore, their value—can be very different depending on where and why they opt in.

Email addresses can be acquired through many sources, including via your website, your store checkout, your blog, a signup request on product packaging or a receipt, an SMS text-to-subscribe sign, your Facebook page, a sweepstakes or contest entry form, co-registration on someone else's website, and on and on. The subscriber who signs up on your homepage is a very different subscriber than the one that signed up because they wanted to enter your sweepstakes.

Tracking the performance of your subscribers by their acquisition source will allow you to see how each is performing and make decisions about which sources to continue, improve, or abandon.

List Building & Profiling

27

Focus on adding engaged subscribers to your list.

Growing your list expands the reach of your messages only if you're adding engaged subscribers. Adding low-quality subscribers to your list who are more likely to ignore or junk your emails than open and act on them is pointless and counterproductive.

Lists that generate too many spam complaints and are bloated with unengaged subscribers have deliverability problems—that is, their emails are diverted to junk folders or blocked altogether by one or more ISPs. In addition to costing time and effort to correct, deliverability problems mean that your emails aren't reaching your engaged subscribers.

Unqualified list growth is a poor goal and an even worse key performance indicator. Engaged list growth, where list size is grown while maintaining or expanding the percentage of engaged subscribers, is a much more effective and safer goal.

List Building & Profiling

28

Recognize that the best email acquisition sources are closest to your shopping and customer service operations.

People who are on your website, using your mobile app, buying your products, shopping at your stores, and talking to your service reps are more familiar with and interested in your brand than those who haven't done those things. That naturally makes such people more valuable and less risky subscribers, and that makes your website, online checkout, store checkout, product packaging and call centers your best email acquisition sources.

Subscriber quality declines and the risk of spam complaints rises the further away you get from these operations. Signups that come from sources outside of your business—such as co-registrations and list rentals—are among the least valuable and most prone to generating spam complaints, but even your social channels might produce subpar subscribers.

List Building & Profiling

29

Don't force people to register as a customer in order to receive promotional emails from you.

The word *register* conjures up visions of long, over-reaching forms and troublesome site passwords in the minds of consumers—and the reward for registering is highly inconsistent. So don't only have your email signup as part of your customer registration form. Also have it as a separate form that you highlight on your homepage and throughout your website.

Signing up for email is a lower bar than customer registration, but if you treat these subscribers well and demonstrate your value over time, you can get the same information from them as someone who registered.

List Building & Profiling

30

Make your email signup forms and links prominent to boost their performance.

Opt-in forms and links convert best when they're prominently placed high on your website where visitors don't have to scroll to find them. Forcing visitors to scroll to find your email opt-in can reduce signups by 50% or more.

To a much smaller degree, opt-ins placed in the right-hand corners tend to outperform those placed in the left-hand corners, because consumers have been trained to expect email opt-in forms in those spots.

Placing your email signup in the header or footer of your website so it appears on every page of your website will also increase signups.

Lightboxes, popovers, and other in-your-face signup requests can also be effective, but be aware that these might annoy some visitors, especially if they are forced to view them repeatedly. Therefore, it's important to test when and how often they are displayed to optimize the overall impact.

List Building & Profiling

31

Tell consumers why they should sign up to receive your emails.

No one wants to join a list, get your emails, or receive your newsletter. People want to receive discounts, product updates, helpful advice, and company news.

Therefore, be sure to sell people on the benefits of subscribing to your email program—whether you have the space to lay out the comprehensive benefits along with images and links to sample emails or whether you only have space for 30 characters.

Keep in mind that the level of convincing that it takes to convert would-be subscribers will vary depending on their acquisition source and the benefits that are of most interest to them. For example, customers who are signing up for email during checkout should take less convincing than people that you're reaching out to via a list rental.

List Building & Profiling

32

Avoid using overly rich signup incentives because they can attract low-quality subscribers.

Coupons, freebies, and other incentives can significantly boost email signups. However, some consumers will subscribe to your emails just for the signup incentive and then turn around and unsubscribe or report your email as spam.

One approach to mitigating this risk is to keep sign-up incentives to a moderate value or ensure that the incentive is only attractive to loyal customers. Another approach is simply to avoid signup incentives altogether to make certain that people are subscribing solely because they want your emails.

Not promoting a signup incentive doesn't mean you can't provide a reward for subscribing in a welcome email.

List Building & Profiling

33

Deliver email signup incentives to the email address provided.

If offered a discount, coupon or freebie on the spot in exchange for their email address, some consumers will give you false email addresses to get the reward. To protect your list quality, deliver any signup incentives to the email address provided. That encourages people to give you their real address and ensures they spell or enter it correctly.

List Building & Profiling

34

Set expectations regarding how many emails you'll be sending subscribers and what content will be in them.

The top two reasons given by subscribers for why they unsubscribe are consistently that they received too many emails and that the emails weren't relevant. Use your signup messaging, signup confirmation page, and welcome emails to set expectations appropriately.

Consider providing images of or links to previous emails as examples of the kind of content you will send. Regarding email frequency, avoid being overly specific so that you have some wiggle room to increase frequency during key selling seasons.

If you offer multiple mailstreams during your opt-in process, be clear about what each one entails.

List Building & Profiling

35

Keep your email signup forms short and simple, and collect additional information after signups.

For most brands, the only piece of information that is absolutely necessary for an email signup is the person's email address. Every bit of information beyond that adds friction to the process and decreases signups.

Opportunities to collect additional information after an email signup include your opt-in confirmation page, preference center, welcome emails, registration forms, online checkouts, sweepstakes entries, and progressive profiling efforts, such as email surveys. As a relationship grows, subscribers will be willing to share more.

If you do require more information at signup for business or compliance reasons, consider breaking the signup process into two or more steps, where each step consists of a short form.

Also consider using a social sign-in for email opt-ins. This convenient option for consumers has the added benefit of providing brands with useful profile information, such as birth date.

List Building & Profiling

36

Recognize that requiring email subscribers to share additional contact information lowers signups significantly.

One of the attractive traits of email marketing is that consumers are fairly willing to share their email addresses with brands. However, people are significantly more guarded when it comes to sharing their mailing address, phone number, and cellphone number because they know doing so exposes them to additional, unwanted marketing communications.

List Building & Profiling

37

Only ask subscribers for information you will use.

Whether on your subscription form, on your opt-in confirmation page, in your welcome email, or further along in the email relationship, asking for information sets the expectation that you'll use it for the subscriber's benefit. Don't ask for information that you think you might use eventually. You can always get that information later and in the meantime you will avoid setting false expectations or dampening the response to a form.

For instance, don't ask subscribers which product categories they are most interested in if you don't plan to use that information to create targeted messages.

List Building & Profiling

38

Explain to subscribers how sharing additional information with you will benefit them.

If you require additional information, tell subscribers how you will use it to their benefit. For instance, if you require their zip code so you can send them news about local events or merchandise carried by stores near them, make that clear. If you require their birth date (perhaps for regulatory reasons) and will use it to send them a special birthday offer, tell them that and make sure you're prepared to follow through.

List Building & Profiling

39

When profiling subscribers, ask them questions that lead you to a clear response.

Try to be as direct as possible when asking about interests and collecting other information during signups, in your preference center or elsewhere. Avoid making assumptions.

For instance, if you want to know if a subscriber is interested in men's or women's apparel, ask them that. Don't ask their gender and assume that men are only interested in buying clothes for themselves.

Similarly, if you have brick-and-mortar stores, don't ask for a subscriber's zip code and assume that their preferred store is the one that's closest to their home. It might be your store that's closest to their workplace or elsewhere, so use their zip code as a starting point but give them the freedom to select a different location.

List Building & Profiling

40

Routinely audit your preference center and acquisition sources to make sure they are up to date and working properly.

Keeping an inventory of all your acquisition sources and tracking their performance is the first step toward identifying problems that might arise from technology and process changes. Regularly checking these subscription pathways for errors is also advised.

Additionally, you should routinely review your signup language and preference center content. For example, make sure you're not offering choices you no longer honor, such as a discontinued newsletter or content choice. If you're asking about equipment, items, or brands your subscribers own, make sure those selections are up to date as well.

Onboarding & Welcome Emails

*"[A welcome email] sets the stage—the tone—
for the rest of the email you will send.
More importantly, a welcome email can
increase your business and help you better
understand your new subscribers."*

—DJ Waldow and Jason Falls, Coauthors of
The Rebel's Guide to Email Marketing

Confirming that a signup was successful is the
bare minimum signup confirmation pages and
welcome emails can do. Because opting in is
strong signal of buyer intent, these onboarding
components reach subscribers when they are
most engaged and most likely to take another
high-value action. Use these touchpoints to
deepen the relationship and drive conversions.

WORDS TO KNOW

onboarding
The process of familiarizing new subscribers with your email program and your brand using your signup confirmation page and welcome emails

welcome email
A message automatically sent to a new subscriber just after they've opted in that welcomes them to your email program and seeks further engagement

welcome email series
Multiple emails automatically sent to a new subscriber over time that seek to maximize engagement

Onboarding & Welcome Emails

41

Use the signup confirmation page as a "pre-welcome message" to continue to engage new subscribers.

When a person signs up to receive your emails, they are reaching out to you and expressing a desire to hear more from you. So don't stop talking after they subscribe.

First, use your signup confirmation page to clearly confirm that the person successfully signed up to receive promotional emails from you, showing them the email address they signed up with so they can verify they entered it correctly.

Second, use it to capitalize on the moment and engage the new subscriber further. Treat it like a pre-welcome message.

For instance, it could be used to ask subscribers to add your email address to their address book, to collect optional preferences and other information, to drive them to key webpages, to educate them about sister brands, or to expose them to your social media channels.

If you plan to send a welcome email immediately, you can tell the subscriber to look for that. Moreover, you can use the signup confirmation page to remind subscribers to check their junk or spam folders if they don't see the welcome email in their inbox.

Although a signup confirmation page could be used in all those ways, focus on one or two of them, because asking subscribers to do too many things at once often lowers response.

Onboarding & Welcome Emails

42

Send a welcome email immediately after signup.

Consumers have been trained to look to their inbox after subscribing, registering, and checking out, so the longer you wait before sending a welcome email the more likely the subscriber will move on to other things. Delays that stretch into days or weeks also increase spam complaints because sometimes people forget that they signed up.

Sending a welcome email immediately maximizes its effectiveness by continuing the momentum of a signup and engaging the subscriber further.

Onboarding & Welcome Emails

43

Send a series of welcome emails to inform and engage new subscribers.

Although sending one welcome email prevents subscribers from abruptly being dropped into your promotional mailstream, you can ease that transition further and quickly engage subscribers more deeply by sending a series of welcome emails.

For instance, you might want to send a new subscriber (1) a rich promotional welcome offer to try to get that first conversion; followed by (2) an email explaining your brand's strengths, such as your standing free shipping offer, exclusive products, and generous return policy; followed by (3) an email discussing the benefits of downloading your mobile app or engaging with you on social media; and concluding with (4) an email reminding them that their welcome offer is expiring in a few days, if they haven't taken advantage of that offer already.

A 3-email welcome series is the most common to send, but the series can range from two all the way up to six or more messages. It all depends on your brand and the information new subscribers need to know.

Onboarding & Welcome Emails

44

Message new subscribers differently depending on their acquisition source and customer history.

Tailor your onboarding messaging to the individual subscriber based on what you know about them and what you know about other subscribers who opted in via the same acquisition source.

For example, people who opt in to your email program through your homepage or while entering a contest are more likely to be new consumers, so you might want to deliver a richer offer to them to encourage them to make their first purchase. Whereas customers who opt in during checkout online or in one of your stores are already familiar with your brand and products, and therefore don't require as rich of an offer to spur their next purchase.

Similarly, if a person signs up for email on your Facebook page, then you shouldn't be pushing them to like you in your welcome emails. Instead, use that opportunity to promote something they're more likely to be unfamiliar with, such as your mobile app or Twitter account.

Additionally, analyze the behavior of your

subscribers by acquisition source and look for patterns of behavior that you can amplify or address in your onboarding messaging.

Onboarding & Welcome Emails

45

Include an unsubscribe link
in your welcome emails.

Some people argue welcome emails don't need to include an unsubscribe link because they are transactional emails, which CAN-SPAM exempts from requiring opt-out links. However, brands should always include an opt-out link in their welcome emails for two reasons:

First, well-crafted welcome emails are promotional emails. These emails should be promoting your products and services, offering deals and discounts, and otherwise trying to get subscribers to convert.

And second, even if you don't take advantage of the promotional power of welcome emails and only send a transactional email that simply confirms the signup and nothing more, denying subscribers the opportunity to unsubscribe only drives them to use the Report Spam button instead.

Similar to using a confirmed opt-in process to protect your list from low-quality acquisition sources, you can use a more prominent unsubscribe link in your welcome email to give regretful subscribers a clear way to opt-out rather than mark your email as spam. A prominent opt-out link can also build trust by signaling to subscribers that you'll make it easy for them to unsubscribe in the future as well.

Making an opt-out link prominent typically involves positioning one in the upper right-corner of the email design opposite your logo, in addition to the usual one positioned at the bottom in the footer of the email. Font size and styling can also ensure that subscribers notice your unsubscribe links.

Onboarding & Welcome Emails

46

Fulfill subscriptions quickly after sending your welcome email(s).

Just like a delay in sending your first welcome email increases spam complaints, so too do delays in fulfilling subscriptions. Minimize this gap as best makes sense.

For instance, if a subscriber signed up for a weekly or monthly email program and your next regular email isn't due for a while, send the most recent email immediately to start demonstrating the value of your program.

Onboarding & Welcome Emails

47

Pay special attention to subscribers during their first weeks on your list, as this is when they are most engaged.

This "honeymoon" period of heightened engagement right after signing up is one of the reasons that sending a welcome email or a series of welcome emails immediately and minimizing subscription fulfillment delays are so important.

However, you may find that other actions are also worth taking, such as sending emails triggered by low initial engagement or a lack of conversions that ask new subscribers more about themselves and their interests so you can send targeted offers.

Envelope Content

"Far from the waterfalls of social media feeds, email and SMS inboxes are more akin to 'to-do' lists that consumers check off, one message at a time. Your email and SMS messages tend to have far greater reach than social media, because every message the user receives creates an impression from its 'from' and subject lines— even if they never open it."
—Jeff Rohrs, Author of *AUDIENCE*

Email interactions generally involve three stages, with reading the envelope content being the first stage. The envelope content consists of the sender or *from* name, the subject line, and the snippet or preview text, if supported by the email client.

WORDS TO KNOW

envelope content
The portion of an email that's visible to subscribers before they open it (i.e., sender name, subject line, etc.)

sender or **from** *name*
The name that appears in the *from* line in an email client

subject line
The text that appears in the *subject* line in an email client

body content or copy
The text, images, and other content inside your email that becomes visible when opened

call-to-action (CTA)
What a message asks a subscriber to do, but more specifically the buttons and links subscribers click to take action

preheader text
HTML text positioned at the very top of an email's body content that is most often used to reinforce or extend the subject line

snippet or preview text
A portion of the first text from inside the email that some email clients display after the subject line in the inbox, when highlighting a new email's arrival, or in other situations

Envelope Content

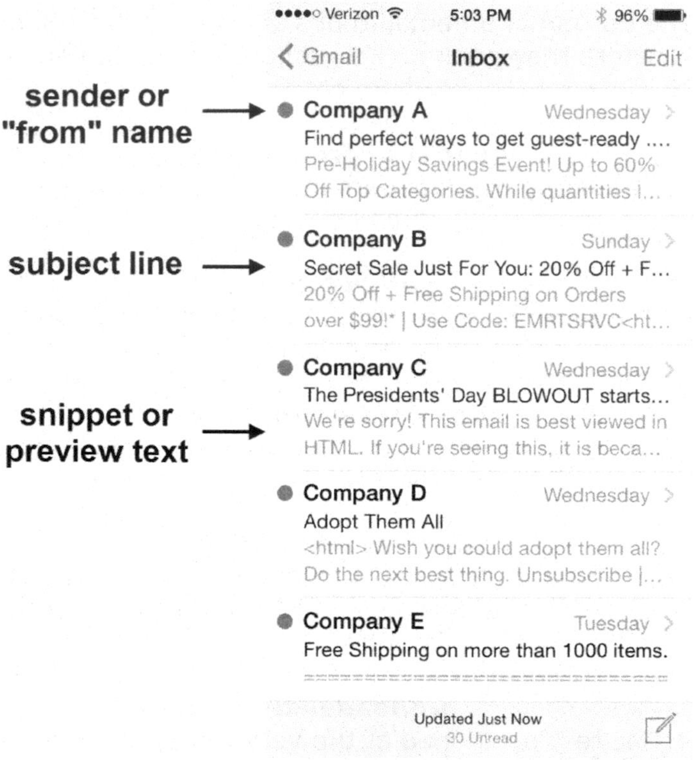

sender or
"from" name ──►

subject line ──►

snippet or
preview text ──►

•••••○ Verizon 🛜   5:03 PM   ✳ 96% ▮▮▮

❮ Gmail   **Inbox**   Edit

● **Company A**   Wednesday ❯
Find perfect ways to get guest-ready ....
Pre-Holiday Savings Event! Up to 60%
Off Top Categories. While quantities l...

● **Company B**   Sunday ❯
Secret Sale Just For You: 20% Off + F...
20% Off + Free Shipping on Orders
over $99!* | Use Code: EMRTSRVC<ht...

● **Company C**   Wednesday ❯
The Presidents' Day BLOWOUT starts...
We're sorry! This email is best viewed in
HTML. If you're seeing this, it is beca...

● **Company D**   Wednesday ❯
Adopt Them All
<html> Wish you could adopt them all?
Do the next best thing. Unsubscribe |...

● **Company E**   Tuesday ❯
Free Shipping on more than 1000 items.

Updated Just Now
30 Unread   ✎

FIGURE 2

Envelope Content

48

Use a recognizable and consistent sender name for your emails.

Although much is written about the power of a good subject line, the identity of the email sender actually has a greater impact on whether the recipient opens it. The sender name, which appears as the *from* name on emails, is the first thing that many email users look at when receiving an email, and many recipients ignore, delete, or mark as spam any emails from senders they don't instantly recognize. (See Fig. 2 on p.104.)

For this reason, using a sender name that subscribers will immediately recognize is critical. For most marketers, that will be your brand name.

Avoid using generic terms such as *newsletter*, *info*, and *customer service*, as well as parent company names, because consumers are not always aware of the relationship between companies.

Also, avoid using the name of your CEO, president, or other officers because people are often not aware of who your leaders are. Moreover, leaders come and go, but your brand name is far less likely to change. The one caveat to this is that B2B marketers might find that using the name of a client's service representative, for instance, is more powerful than the name of their company.

To ensure that your entire sender name displays, keep it to 20 characters or less.

After you decide on the appropriate sender name to use, always use that name so subscribers are trained to look for it. Don't change it for special one-off emails. If you want to indicate that an email contains a special message from your CEO, for example, use the subject line to indicate that.

Envelope Content

49

Keep your subject lines short but still coherent and descriptive.

People are in a hurry while they scan their inboxes and decide which emails to open. Overly long subject lines are a turnoff to many consumers and don't lead to more clicks or conversions among those who do open.

At the other end of the spectrum, very short subject lines often generate higher-than-average open rates, but lower-than-average click rates. These subject lines tend to be more intriguing and mysterious but, as a result, attract curious subscribers rather than subscribers who are most likely to respond to the calls-to-action in the email. Additionally, using too many vague, short subject lines might cause fewer subscribers to open your emails over time because the email content has repeatedly disappointed them.

Although growing smartphone readership will continue to put downward pressure on subject line length, the sweet spot appears to be in the neighborhood of 20 to 40 characters, which generally produces above average conversions and clicks, as well as opens. That range includes enough characters to clearly convey two or more attributes of the email's content—including the topic, value, urgency, and relevance to the subscriber—while staying true to your brand's voice.

If you decide to use a subject line that's more than 40 characters long, consider frontloading it with your keywords and main call-to-action to limit the impact of it being truncated.

Be aware that word choice can affect perceived subject line length because several long words can be easier to read than a bunch of short words.

Of all the email elements covered in this book, subject lines are the most frequently tested—and rightfully so. The perfect subject line lies at the intersection of your message, brand, and audience—that is, what you want to communicate, how your brand typically communicates, and which kinds of communications your subscribers tend to be most receptive to. Finding that point requires a deep understanding of all three elements, which is a process that's as much art as it is science.

Envelope Content

50

Recognize that an unopened email delivers a brand impression and call-to-action through its sender name and subject line.

Although every marketer wants every single one of their emails opened, very few subscribers are that engaged. Even so, emails still generate value when they go unopened by subscribers who at least occasionally engage with your emails.

First, a subscriber who deletes an email unopened is still exposed to your brand name in the *from* line, which helps keep your brand top of mind and might prompt interactions in other online or offline channels.

Second, if the subject line is clear about what action you want subscribers to take, it has an even better chance of prompting interactions in other channels or generating word of mouth. For instance, a subject line about summer apparel might serve as a general reminder for the subscriber to stop by their local store to refresh their summer wardrobe. And including a promo code in a subject line might spur a subscriber to make a purchase without even needing to open the email.

And third, the subject line can affect subscriber interest in opening future emails. For example, if the subject line promotes a good deal but the recipient is just not in the market to shop at the moment, the savings message still reaffirms the subscriber's belief in the value of your emails and would keep them interested in future emails.

For those reasons, avoid relying too much on vague and mysterious subject lines to generate opens. Over time, this can erode trust by making subscribers feel misled by your subject lines and forced to open your emails to find out what's inside.

Instead, try to be descriptive, using keywords connected to the primary message and maybe an important secondary message. A subject line should help subscribers decide whether opening the email will be a good use of their time. Respecting your subscribers' time makes them less likely to tune you out and more likely to stay subscribed.

Envelope Content

51

Measure the success of a subject line by how well it drives clicks and conversions.

Just because subscribers sequentially interact with your subject line, your email, and then your landing page content before converting, don't be tempted to believe that subject lines only affect opens.

A good subject line is one that predisposes subscribers who open to be receptive to the content of the email and ultimately convert at a higher rate. Put another way, a good subject line preselects openers so that those subscribers who open an email are the ones mostly likely to be interested in its contents. Therefore a subject line that produces fewer opens but more conversions is preferable to one that produces more opens but fewer conversions.

When evaluating subject lines, also be sure to look at unsubscribe and spam complaint rates, because you always want to keep these rates low.

Envelope Content

52

Use snippet text like a "second subject line" to support and extend your subject line.

Snippet or preview text plays a unique role in email design because while it's technically body copy, it's also sometimes envelope copy. That's because some email clients display a small portion of the first body copy after the subject line in the inbox, when highlighting a new email's arrival, or in other situations. (See Fig. 2 on p.104.)

Make the most of snippet text by including preheader text, which is HTML text positioned at the very top of an email's body content. Ensure that it supports and extends the subject line of your email. In other words, treat it like a second subject line.

Avoid having your preheader repeat the subject line and try to keep administrative preheader text from showing up as snippet text. For instance, preheaders might also include links to view the web-hosted version of the email, to visit your social media pages, to update preferences and to unsubscribe. If you include any of those options in your preheader, make sure they're not among the first 70 or so characters in your email as to avoid squandering the opportunity provided by snippet text.

Similarly, don't ask your subscribers to add your email address to their address book or Safe Sender list in the preheader of every email you send. Make that request on your signup confirmation page and in your welcome email series. If subscribers haven't done it after being asked a few times, they're unlikely to ever do it and you're just wasting valuable screen real estate by endlessly asking.

Consider including a more direct call-to-action in your preheader text by linking all or a portion of it to the primary landing page for the email so subscribers can easily click through and take action after they open the message.

Email Design & Body Content

"There's really only one central principle of good content: it should be appropriate for your business, for your users, and for its context. Appropriate in its method of delivery, in its style and structure, and above all in its substance."

—Erin Kissane, Author of *The Elements of Content Strategy*

When a subscriber opens your email, they've reached the second stage of email interaction: reading the body content of your email.

For some brands, this is the end game, but for the vast majority, this is just one step closer to the goal of generating a conversion. Effective email design and compelling body copy help propel subscribers on to the final stage of email interaction.

WORDS TO KNOW

email template
Preformatted email file that includes all the elements you want to appear in every email and spots for content that changes from email to email

rendering
How an email client translates an email's coding and displays the email

responsive email design
Advanced design techniques that produce versions or renderings of an email that are optimized for particular screen resolutions or email clients

mobile-aware or scalable email design
Basic design techniques that create a single email that functions well across a range of screen sizes, but is deferential to smartphones

desktop-centric design
Design techniques that create emails optimized for viewing on large monitors, typically with small, tightly clustered links and buttons

image blocking
When ISPs or subscribers don't allow the images in an email to load

defensive design
Design techniques that allow an email to communicate its message effectively when images are blocked

alt *text*
Text coded into an *<img>* tag that is displayed
when the image is blocked and when recipients
mouse over the image, although support is
not consistent

HTML or system text
Text from a limited number of fonts that are
universally or widely supported across email clients

graphical text
Text that is part of an image

header
The upper portion of an email that includes your
brand's logo

navigation bar
A row of links to important pages on your website

primary message or content block, or hero
The main message of an email, which is usually
positioned at the top of the email and larger than
other messages in the email

secondary message or content block
The other message(s) in an email, usually following
and smaller than the primary message

product grid
A multi-column and usually multi-row layout where
each grid cell contains a product image and other
information, such as product name, brand, and price

Anatomy of a Typical Email

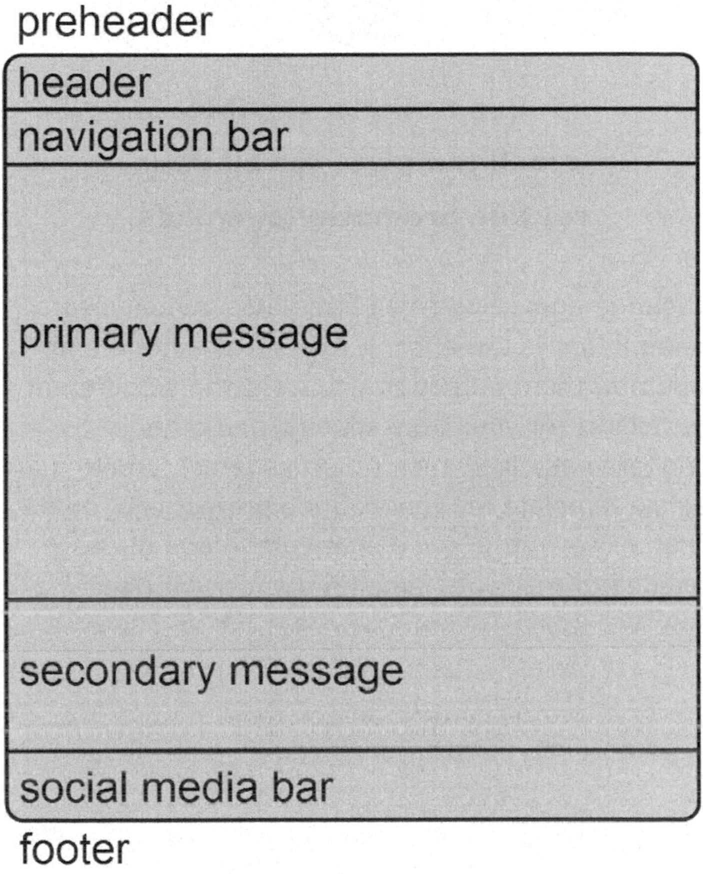

preheader

header
navigation bar

primary message

secondary message

social media bar

footer

FIGURE 3

Email Design & Body Content

53

Use a single, flexible email template for all your routine promotional emails.

Creating numerous email templates invites errors and multiplies the effort it takes to maintain and optimize them. Although you want to use different templates for your transactional and other triggered emails (which I discuss later), create a single template for your routine promotional emails that allows you to swap elements in and out as needed to make any email message you need.

Email Design & Body Content

54

Design your emails to render well and function properly across a wide range of platforms and devices.

Very few subscribers will open your emails more than once, so make sure your emails display well on both smartphones and desktops—and everything in between.

In fact, a considerable percentage of email users would rather unsubscribe than try to navigate emails that render poorly on their preferred email client or device.

Support for HTML and CSS coding varies across email clients and browsers, and support can change without notice, so it is important to use a rendering preview tool or routinely view your emails in a wide range of email clients to check for inconsistencies.

This issue has become more critical as an increasing percentage of subscribers read email on their smartphones. Small screens can make it difficult to easily read and engage with promotional emails that are not designed with mobile devices in mind. For this reason, it's highly recommended that you use mobile-aware design or responsive design for your emails, because you can no longer expect subscribers who have lackluster experiences with emails on mobile devices to save and reopen them later on laptops or desktops. The vast majority will just hit Delete.

Mobile-aware design involves basic techniques to create a single email that functions well across a range of screen sizes, but is deferential to smartphones. Those techniques include:

- Employing a single-column layout (two-column product grids are okay);

- Using large text (at least 12 pt), images, and buttons;

- Spacing out links and buttons—including those in navigation, social, and administrative bars—so subscribers can tap them accurately; and

- Using high contrast values and colors for ease of reading outdoors and in other less-than-ideal settings.

Responsive design has become a general term for a basket of advanced techniques that produce versions or renderings of an email that are optimized for particular screen resolutions or email clients. Whether it's fluid, liquid, adaptive, truly responsive, or powered by live content, these techniques involve extra email design and coding—and often the creation of two or more versions of an email. However, the result is email messaging that looks good and functions properly on a range of devices.

Consult with your ESP or an email design specialist to determine the best design approach for your brand.

The growing use of smartphones to read emails opens up other new email design opportunities as well. For instance, make phone numbers in your emails tappable so subscribers can instantly make that call. Additionally, mobile apps can be used as landing pages, instead of just websites.

Email Design & Body Content

55

Design your emails so they convey their message even when images are blocked.

Many email clients block images by default and some subscribers don't turn images on, so relying too heavily on images to communicate your message can be a losing strategy. Defend against image-blocking ruining your message by using two common defensive design techniques:

- Adding *alt* text to your image coding
- Using HTML or system text as much as feasible instead of embedding text in your images

The *alt* text of an image generally appears when the image is blocked and when recipients mouse over enabled images, although support isn't consistent across email clients. If an image contains graphical text, use the *alt* text to replicate all or some of that text so recipients can read it when images are not enabled. You can create emphasis and better mimic the images-on version of your email by applying style settings to the image tag to change the font size and color of your *alt* text, although support is again inconsistent.

HTML text should be limited to just a small number of popular font families—including Arial,

Courier New, Georgia, Times New Roman, and Verdana—but these fonts are universally supported. In most cases, the fonts can also be styled in different sizes and colors.

Use HTML text at the very top of your emails before the header to create preheader text, which most often communicates the primary call-to-action of the email or builds on the content of the subject line. HTML text can also be used for your navigation bar links; throughout your primary and secondary messaging blocks, particularly for headlines, coupon codes, and calls-to-action; and in a product grid. And, of course, HTML text should be used for all footer text and administrative links, such as your mailing address and unsubscribe link.

Using these defensive design tactics allows for the graceful degradation of your email message and is especially critical in the first emails that a consumer receives from you, such as welcome and transactional emails, when your images are most likely to be turned off.

While you shouldn't ignore image blocking as a design consideration, you shouldn't let it deter you from using images either. Most B2C brands send emails that are at least 50% image-based. And lifestyle, aspirational, and high-end brands send emails that are almost entirely image-based, since pictures are key to conveying the appeal of these brands' products. Use defensive design thoughtfully, but don't let it cause you to sacrifice how you project your brand image.

WORDS TO KNOW

preview or reading pane
A window in some email clients that allows subscribers to view a smaller portion of an email than if the email were opened in its own window

above the fold
The portion of an email that displays before a subscriber scrolls

below the fold
The portion of an email that displays only after a subscriber scrolls

newsjacking
Leveraging the popularity of a news story, event, or cultural phenomena to promote yourself or your company

share with your network (SWYN)
Functionality that allows subscribers to add content from your email to their social media timeline so their network of friends, family members, and other connections can see it

forward to a friend (FTAF)
Providing a link in your email that takes subscribers to a form that allows them to forward all or a portion of your email or a particular message promoted in your email to one or more people that they know

Email Design & Body Content

56

Design your emails with a clear content hierarchy so they can be easily scanned by subscribers.

Subscribers don't read emails; they scan them. So make it easy for subscribers to skim your email content by creating a clear hierarchy of content and calls-to-action (CTAs).

Use strong headlines that are substantially larger than the text that falls under them. The primary message block, or hero, should be larger than any secondary content blocks and should immediately, or at least closely, follow the header and navigation bar. Moreover, the key CTAs should be large and ideally in the form of buttons so they stand out.

Using phrases and bulleted items rather than full sentences makes email content easy to scan. If you have to use full sentences, avoid blocks of text that are more than five lines long because large blocks of text discourage readers.

In most cases, your email is just a gateway to your website or some other final destination, so you don't need to include every detail of an offer. You just need to convey the highlights in a way that compels subscribers to click through and get the rest of the details.

Email Design & Body Content

57

Design your email content so it can be viewed in screen-sized chunks.

Don't design your emails as you would posters or store signage. Unless a particular email is small, subscribers don't see an entire email at once, but rather in screen-sized chunks while they scroll through it.

How much of an email is displayed at one time varies by device and email client, and is considerably smaller when a subscriber is using a preview or reading pane, which shows less of the email at a time than if it were opened in its own window. However, a good rule of thumb is to design your emails assuming that subscribers will only see about 400 pixels of height at a time.

Images are less affected by this constraint than text is. Design your emails so that logical groups of text are visible on a single screen so they can be read at once.

For text-heavy emails and emails with several message blocks, create clean breaks between content blocks by using containers, lines or rules, and white space.

For image-heavy emails, be mindful of how a subscriber would scroll through the email. Large images that take several screens to scroll through can create intrigue, encourage subscribers to scroll, and highlight the details of the image, but be strategic about where you place copy and calls-to-action. Near the top and near the bottom tend to be effective.

Email Design & Body Content

58

Pay extra attention to the top portion of your email that appears above the fold and ensure it's well-branded.

The email content that appears above the fold on that first screen-sized chunk is the most critical because some subscribers will not scroll down to see the content that's below the fold. Again, assume that your subscribers will only see 400-pixel-tall chunks of your email at a time on average.

The standard promotional email begins with preheader text followed by the header, which includes your brand's logo. Next is a navigation bar that provides links to key pages on your website, and then the primary content block that includes your main message. (See Fig. 3 on p.117.)

Having your logo visible above the fold is essential as it provides additional confirmation of who the sender is. Most marketers position their logo on the left side of the header, so it's seen immediately as subscribers scan downward from the left side of the screen. Centered logos are less common but also an option, although there is a risk of them being cut off in email clients that don't scale emails down to fit the subscriber's screen.

Avoid having multiple lines of preheader text or an overly large logo because these push your primary message farther down in the email so that less of it appears above the fold.

Similar to the navigation bar on your website, email nav bars can serve as a significant source of clicks by offering a quick path to important pages on your website.

Just because the top portion of your email is the most read, don't try to cram too much content up top. Content still needs room to breathe. But you'll probably want to position headlines and other key text toward the top of your primary content block so at least part of it appears above the fold.

Email Design & Body Content

59

Design your emails so they are harmonious with, but don't exactly mirror, your website's design.

You should use consistent branding and general style across all your channels, including email, but recognize that every channel is different.

For example, emails enjoy less design freedom than websites because of inferior and inconsistent coding support across the various email clients. Emails have less screen real estate to work with than websites because emails often share the screen with inbox navigation and sometimes ads. And subscribers often act differently than website visitors because they are more engaged with your brand and because emails aren't usually intended to deliver a complete experience without clicking through to a website.

For those reasons, don't shrink your website design and use it in your emails. Instead, design your emails so they incorporate key branding elements from your website while being optimized for the email channel. Use the same color scheme, but be flexible on the layout and design elements, such as fonts. For instance, opt for a widely supported HTML font rather than the exact font you use on your website.

Navigation bars are another area where you're better off using a derivative of what's on your website. Because emails are generally narrower than websites, you typically have room for fewer links. Generally, mobile-friendly email designs have nav bars with two to four links and desktop-optimized designs have six to eight.

Given these limitations, think about the nav links that will be of most interest to your email subscribers. Also, consider changing up your nav bar links from one email to the next in order to support the primary message of each one.

Email Design & Body Content

60

Create an email content calendar to aid in resource allocation and content and design planning.

Many marketers start working on an email weeks or even months before the send date—especially those that involve extra design work, web or IT resources, or coordination with other groups.

Having an email content calendar helps you allocate time for planning and executing mails. It also ensures you retain an overview of your content, so you produce the right mix of content and put the appropriate focus on key selling periods. For instance, some brands start planning their holiday email promotions as early as July.

Having a content calendar also lets you plan for occasions when you need to have multiple content options available to respond to potential outcomes, such as promoting Super Bowl champion gear, albums of Grammy winners, or products pegged to whether the groundhog saw his shadow.

You can't plan for everything, however. Sometimes, news and other events provide great marketing opportunities. Give yourself the flexibility to participate in newsjacking and leverage current events to promote your products and engage customers.

Email Design & Body Content

61

Provide context for products featured in your emails.

Don't assume that subscribers know what your products are for, how to use them, or the differences between similar products. Provide context for your products to help inspire subscribers to buy and to remove barriers to buying.

For instance, an apparel retailer might show the same blouse used in two outfits, one dressed up and one dressed down, to show its versatility. An electronics retailer might link to an article or blog post that explains the different kinds of HDTV display technologies. And a home improvement retailer might promote a video that demonstrates all the uses of a power washer.

In other words, think of ways to strengthen the appeal of your promotional content by weaving in elements of content marketing. All brands should think of themselves as publishers.

Email Design & Body Content

62

Give your customers and other people a voice in your emails.

Consumers trust what others do and say more than they trust what companies say, so give your customers, outside experts, media outlets, bloggers, celebrities, and others a presence in your emails.

Consider promoting top-selling, top-rated, most-liked, most-tweeted, and most-pinned items, and including pictures, videos, testimonials, reviews, tweets, and other content provided by customers. Poll your customers and include the results in an email.

Also, consider including advice, curated product assortments, and other content from outside experts, as well as pointing out media coverage of your products. The voice of your staffers can also ring more true than anonymous, disembodied corporate content.

Email Design & Body Content

63

Offer subscribers non-promotional content and calls-to-action.

Although the goal of your email program is likely to generate sales, that doesn't mean that every message has to scream, *Buy Now!*

Subscribers are not always in the market to buy your products, so incessantly asking them to buy can be off-putting and cause them to tune you out. Keep your subscribers engaged when they're not in the market by including non-promotional content in your emails.

The soft sell can be surprisingly effective, because it can engage, inspire, and motivate subscribers to buy when they didn't consider themselves in the market. This approach can move a subscriber down the sales funnel, too, making them more receptive to hard sell messaging in the future.

For those reasons, balance your promotional content with some educational, instructional, editorial, social, and inspirational content. This could take the form of surveys and polls that give you progressive profiling data, updates on social media activity, information about your charity or conservation efforts, or season's greetings and other messages of thanks.

Email Design & Body Content

64

Use faster channels to help determine the content of your emails.

Improve the results of your email marketing campaigns by incorporating learnings from faster channels like site search, pay-per-click (PPC) search campaigns, and Twitter and other fast-moving social media.

For instance, look at the terms that visitors are putting into your website's search box and use popular terms in your subject lines or body copy. You can also fine-tune the landing page of a PPC search campaign before using it for an email campaign or use insights from PPC search ad headlines and body copy for subject lines and preheader text. And tweets that generate high engagement should be used to inform subject lines and headline copy.

The inverse is also possible. You can use the results of your email campaigns to inform slower channels. For instance, you can test product images in emails and use the winners in your upcoming catalog.

Email Design & Body Content

65

Make your calls-to-action clear
in language and positioning.

If you want subscribers to do something, tell them by using direct language in your calls-to-action (CTAs). If you want them to buy a product, use a *Buy Now* CTA rather than the generic and less compelling *Click Here* CTA—which is also increasingly inappropriate because of the rise of touchscreens.

Similarly, place your CTAs so that they punctuate the copy that's associated with it. For example, if you want subscribers to share a discount code in an email with their friends and family on Twitter, Facebook, and other social networks, place a share-with-your-network (SWYN) link with a *Share This Deal* CTA right next to the discount code just as you'd place a *Buy Now* button next to product information.

Email Design & Body Content

66

Offer subscribers many paths to click through from an email.

Generally, when we talk about calls-to-action (CTAs), we're referring to buttons and text links. However, subscribers have a much broader definition of a CTA.

They see the logo in your header, the headlines, and any image in your email (whether it is a product shot or not), as a CTA that they'll try to click. Make the most of their interest by making as many of these elements clickable as possible.

That said, don't cluster non-identical links too closely together because subscribers reading your email on tablets and, in particular, smartphones might have difficulty accurately selecting a link with their finger.

Email Design & Body Content

67

Don't limit your email calls-to-action to online only.

Email can drive subscribers to act offline just as effectively as it can drive them to act online, so don't shy away from promoting store events and other happenings. In fact, the increase in mobile email reading makes offline calls-to-action more effective, because you can increasingly reach subscribers when they are out and about.

Subscribers are more likely to be out of the home on weekends, during the warmer months, and especially on big shopping days like Thanksgiving Eve, Thanksgiving Day, Black Friday, and the day after Christmas. Those are all occasions to be more mindful of mobile readers and to consider including store-only deals, mobile coupons, and store-specific information such as hours in your emails.

WORDS TO KNOW

weight
The file size of the HTML coding of an email

loaded or total weight
The file size of the HTML coding of an email plus the total file size of all images used in the email

animated gif
An image file that displays multiple images sequentially over time, sometimes in a loop

static or still image
An image that doesn't change over time, unlike an animated gif

cinemagraph
A picture composed of both static images and one or more animated gifs, which give motion, often subtle, to a small portion of the overall picture

video gif
A compressed, streaming animated gif capable of video-quality frame rates

live content
Images and other email content that vary based on when the email is opened, what kind of device it's opened on, and other factors

recovery module
A secondary content block usually positioned right before the footer that contains many links to different product categories, brands, or other areas of your website that is designed to appeal to subscribers who were uninterested in the other calls-to-action in the email

social media bar
A row of social media icons that link to your brand's pages on those social media sites

footer
The HTML text at the bottom of an email that includes the promotional fine print, legal language, unsubscribe link, mailing address, and other details

Email Design & Body Content

68

Keep the weight of your emails reasonable to avoid long load times and deliverability issues.

When the file size of an email message is too large, ISPs might display only a portion of the message or block it completely. Very large emails also load more slowly for subscribers, especially if they use mobile devices, which might cause them to hit Delete in frustration.

As network and device speeds change in the years ahead, guidelines and limits on email file sizes will likely change. For now, aim to keep the weight of the HTML coding of your emails to 60 KB or less—and be very wary of exceeding 100 KB.

Note that this doesn't include the file size of web-hosted images associated with an email, which could be an additional several hundred kilobytes—or even more for graphic-heavy messages. Keep the loaded or total weight—email coding plus images—to less than 800 KB.

Email Design & Body Content

69

Do not include attachments on your commercial emails.

Consumers are very hesitant to open attachments because of the risk of viruses and other malicious payloads. For that reason, and because attachments often dramatically increase the weight of your email, ISPs and corporate email servers are more likely to block your emails if you include attachments.

Instead, host any PDF coupons, documents, or other files on the web and link to them from the email or link to a webpage that lets subscribers download these materials and then easily navigate to other parts of your website.

Email Design & Body Content

70

Use motion selectively
in emails to engage subscribers.

Because most email content is static, movement really stands out in an email.

Animated gifs are the most common mechanism for adding motion to email because most email clients support them. Animation can be used to demonstrate how a product works, show color or style variations of a product, draw attention to a call-to-action or secondary message, or add some fun and whimsy to a design.

Be mindful of the size and frame counts of your animated gifs to prevent the file size from getting too large. And avoid using too many animations in a single email because they can make the message seem overly busy and distract the recipient.

Luckily, cinemagraphs and other small animations can be just as effective as large ones. And many very effective animated gifs get away with containing only three to five frames.

Some email clients block animated gifs and only show the first frame of the animation. You should plan for that possibility by using an image that can stand on its own as your first frame. Often, that means placing what you'd typically consider the last frame of your animation first.

You can also use HTML5 video, video gifs, live content, and other mechanisms to add motion to your email designs. These tools are best reserved for content where you're showing complex motion. Support for the various video methods is inconsistent across email clients, so make sure that you incorporate fallbacks, such as animated gifs and static images, for those email clients that don't support your selected form of video.

Video in email can be quite tricky to implement, so it's best to consult with your ESP or an email design specialist to determine the best approach for your brand.

Email Design & Body Content

71

Don't include sound effects or auto-play videos with sound enabled by default in your emails.

People expect the internet to be a largely silent experience unless they press a Play button. That's even truer of their expectations around email, especially as more emails are read on mobile devices in stores and restaurants, in meetings, during presentations, and at other times when sounds might be embarrassing and otherwise unwelcome.

Avoid the temptation to use sound as a tactic to stand out from the crowd.

Email Design & Body Content

72

Don't avoid creating long emails because you think subscribers won't scroll.

Although higher email frequencies and more consumers reading emails on smartphones are driving many marketers to send shorter emails, subscribers will still engage with longer emails. Beyond having compelling content, marketers can use several techniques to encourage subscribers to scroll and, in doing so, expose the recipient to more of the content in your emails.

First, use a single-column rather than a two column format to make it easier for subscribers to scroll. Including product grids generally doesn't impede scrolling, as long as the grid isn't more than two columns on mobile devices and four columns on desktops.

Second, look for opportunities to use an S-curve layout, where an image on the left and text on the right is followed on the next row down by an image on the right and text on the left, and so on. Subscribers often find this arrangement easier to read than having all images on the left and all text on the right, or vice versa.

Third, use images with strong vertical or

sloping lines, as subscribers' eyes naturally follow these lines, especially if the image is only partially revealed. For instance, if subscribers see the top of a Christmas tree or part of a necklace chain, many will be intrigued enough to scroll to see the entire tree or necklace.

And fourth, consistently place some high-value content deep in your emails. If you stick with a consistent layout, subscribers will be trained to look for certain types of content throughout your email. For instance, if you always place a coupon at the bottom of your email—and perhaps call attention to it with a short message in your header or in a small banner right below your header— subscribers will learn that they have to scroll down to find that coupon.

When you send long emails, be thoughtful about the content you place at the very bottom before the footer, as that content tends to attract more attention than the content that falls in the middle.

You can determine if your email content is scroll-worthy by looking at a heatmap of where the clicks are in an email. If there are little to no clicks on the content toward the bottom of your emails, then they are too long or you need better content.

Email Design & Body Content

73

Don't expect subscribers to scroll back to the top of your emails.

Expecting subscribers to scroll to the bottom of even very long emails is reasonable; however, expecting them to scroll back to the top is not. For that reason, consider using content with a high link density at the bottom of your emails to give subscribers many alternatives to the message blocks higher up.

One tactic is to include a recovery module, which is a content block that contains many links to different product categories, product sub-categories, price points, or brands, for instance. Sometimes recovery modules are related to the theme of the email, but other times they just promote sale or clearance items in various product categories.

Another tactic is to repeat your navigation bar before your footer or elsewhere in the email.

Email Design & Body Content

74

Include links to your social media pages and your mobile app in your emails.

Email subscribers are among your best customers and you can make them even better customers if you can also engage them through social media, your blog, and your mobile app. Providing links to these channels in your emails is a constant reminder of other ways to interact with your brand and see what other customers are saying.

Most marketers include these links right before their footer in a social media bar, but some include them in their header to the right of their logo. Above the fold space is precious, so if you include these links in your header, make sure they are performing well enough to earn that position.

If you include both share-with-your-network (SWYN) links and social community links in your emails, differentiating them by prefacing your SWYN links with *Share:* and your social community links with *Follow Us:* or something similar.

Email Design & Body Content

75

Don't place anything important after your footer copy because subscribers are unlikely to see it.

Subscribers have been trained to stop scrolling when they reach email footers, where you place your offer exclusions and other legalese, administrative links like unsubscribe links, and mailing address for CAN-SPAM compliance. Anything positioned after your footer is likely to go unseen.

Email Design & Body Content

76

Use a consistent email design, but don't be afraid to deviate from it occasionally.

Having a consistent email design is brand-building, makes you more recognizable in the inbox, and creates familiarity. However, it can also give the impression that all your messages are equally important. Monotony can lull subscribers into paying less attention to you.

Significantly changing your email design on a one-off basis every once in a while can deliver a "wake-up slap" that gets your subscribers' complete attention again.

Occasions where it might make sense to deviate from your usual email design include a major product launch, entry into a new product category, collaboration with another brand, a charity effort, a big social media or mobile campaign, or a win-back campaign aimed at reengaging subscribers who haven't clicked or converted in a long time.

In these situations, consider one of these options for deviating from your usual email template in a significant way:

- Depart from your usual color palette
- Drop your navigation bar and similar links to draw attention to your primary message
- Send a plain text email to express urgency
- Break the grid, where a portion of an image extends past the usual boundaries of the email
- Use a shallow but wide creative where subscribers have to scroll to the right instead of down

Although some consider these tactics breaking the rules, I consider it a rule to mix things up periodically to keep things interesting and create emphasis.

Email Design & Body Content

77

Keep a swipe file of your most successful email campaigns and components to inspire future campaigns.

A swipe file is a record of your emails, subject lines, calls-to-action, content blocks, landing pages, and other email elements that performed really well. You can return to this file for learnings and inspiration.

For instance, a swipe file helps you keep track of subject line arrangements, keywords, and offers that your subscribers responded to best. It works the same for email designs, allowing you to model new designs off previously successful ones. You can even reuse past winners, although it's best to reimagine, reskin, or further optimize them.

Monitoring what your competitors and others are doing with their email programs is also a good way to get new ideas that you can then test and make your own. You can do that by signing up for their emails yourself or by using a service that aggregates and categorizes commercial emails, making monitoring easier.

Seasonality

"Marketers need to take a customer-centric approach to their holiday strategy, leveraging the data they have about their customers to individualize the customer journey."

—Wacarra Yeomans, Senior Director of Creative Services, Oracle Marketing Cloud

Consumers behave differently when they're buying for others, and that's especially truly during November and December during the run up to Christmas. You should adapt the appearance, content, and frequency of your emails to match those changes.

WORDS TO KNOW

seasonality
Related to an upcoming or current season, holiday, or buying occasion

holiday header
A temporary, holiday-themed header design that supports the seasonal messaging of your emails

gift services footer
A secondary content block that is typically positioned just before the footer that pulls together links to gift guides, order-by deadlines, return policies, and other important seasonal buying information

secondary navigation bar
Typically positioned right below your standard nav bar, this nav bar provides deeper navigation into one of your standard nav bar links, links to seasonal merchandise and content, or links that support the primary message or theme of the email

Seasonality

78

Signal the arrival of the holiday season and other seasonal events by altering your email designs.

Stores hang garlands, decorate Christmas trees, and put up lots of red and green signage to indicate that the holiday season has arrived. Email designs should similarly signal to subscribers that it's time to start thinking about gift buying.

You can accomplish this in a few different ways. First, add seasonal imagery to your email designs, particularly to your header because it appears above the fold.

Second, add a link to your navigation bar that directs subscribers to seasonal merchandise or your gift guide. You might also consider adding a holiday-themed secondary navigation bar dedicated entirely to promoting your seasonal merchandise and content.

And third, add a gift services footer, which pulls together links to gift guides, order-by deadlines, return policies, and other important seasonal buying information into a single content block.

Seasonality

79

Make your opt-in forms, welcome emails, and other email marketing components seasonally relevant.

In addition to changing your email design and content in response to seasonality, you should adjust other aspects of your email program, too, including your opt-in forms, welcome emails, transactional emails, preference center, and unsubscribe page.

For instance, the email signup call-to-action on your homepage could be changed in November to read, *Don't miss our exclusive Black Friday and Cyber Monday email deals*. That makes for a much more compelling call-to-action because the value statement is much more pointed and urgent with those two key shopping days approaching.

Similarly, you could also add a Valentine's Day gift services footer to your order confirmation and shipping confirmation emails in January and early February. This will spur additional purchases from customers who were buying things for themselves.

Seasonality

80

Send subscribers more email when they are in the market or otherwise predisposed to take action.

Subscribers tolerate—and even welcome—more email when it arrives at a time that's helpful to them.

For instance, retailers wisely send more promotional emails during the holiday season, knowing that their subscribers are actively looking for gift ideas and making many purchases. Similarly, many charities and other nonprofits send more email toward the end of the year, knowing that many people make most of their charitable donations just before the end of the calendar year for tax purposes.

However, as you increase email frequency during holiday periods, keep a close eye on how your subscribers respond. If engagement dips and spam complaints and unsubscribes rise too much, that's a sign to back down.

Seasonality

81

Message your subscribers differently during the holiday season.

Consumers use email differently during November and December than they do the other 10 months of the year. During the holiday season, people are extremely busy, travel more, might have to deal with bad weather, and have longer-than-usual lists of things to do. In short, they're more stressed.

They turn to promotional emails to make their lives easier by helping them find great gifts at great prices—and that's about it. Marketers can adjust their email content by simplifying, reducing, or eliminating video and social media calls-to-action, contests, advice and lifestyle content, and other content that requires too much of a time commitment from subscribers. The holiday season is the time to simplify messaging.

It's also a time to increase customer service messaging, such as clarifying return policies, promoting order-by deadlines, and highlighting store hours.

Seasonality

82

Recognize that once-a-year gift-buying makes subscribers' interests less predictable during the holiday season.

Consumers are mostly buying for others during the holiday season, so downplay or disregard content preferences and previous browse and purchase behavior when making decisions about what content to send individual subscribers.

Instead, promote a wider selection of products and product categories and direct subscribers to a gift guide that helps them find gifts by interest, gender, age, price, or other variables. Also, consider promoting fewer product category sales in favor of more sitewide sales.

Similarly, be wary of using the behavior of subscribers in December to send them targeted messages in January.

Targeting & Personalization

"Mass marketers develop a product and try to find customers for that product. But 1:1 marketers develop a customer and try to find products for that customer."

—Don Peppers and Martha Rogers,
Coauthors of *The One to One Future*

Although "one size fits all" broadcast emails will always be at least a slim majority of the messaging email marketers send, the effectiveness of such messages is steadily declining. Consumers expect more. They expect marketers to listen to them—both to what they say and how they act—and respond with messages that are tailored to their interests.

This takes more effort than broadcast emails, but your subscribers will handsomely reward your efforts. Targeted emails often generate results that are multiple times better than those of broadcast emails, and have the added benefit of lower unsubscribe and spam complaint rates.

With targeted messages on the rise, think of your program's role less as email marketing and more as providing an email-powered personal shopper program that offers thoughtful recommendations, helpful advice, and responsive customer service.

WORDS TO KNOW

targeting
Sending the right message to the right subscriber at the right time

expressed preferences
The topics, activities, and other things that subscribers tell you they are interested in

implied preferences
The topics, activities, and other things that subscribers indicate they are interested in based on their interactions with your brand

broadcast email
An email that is sent to all subscribers

segmentation
Sending a particular message to only those subscribers who are likely to respond based on their geography, demographics, behavior, or other factors; or sending the same message to subscribers at different times based on their time zone or geography

dynamic content
A portion of an email that contains different content for different groups of subscribers or individuals based on their geography, demographics, behavior, or other factors

personalization
Including information that's unique to the recipient in the subject line or body copy of an email

Targeting & Personalization

83

Recognize that what subscribers do is more important than what they say.

Expressed preferences—what subscribers tell you they are interested in during signup, through progressive profiling, and at other times—can become outdated rather quickly. People are not always the best judges of their own interests and sometimes their plans, intentions, and circumstances change suddenly.

Expressed preferences are a good starting point, but are trumped by implied preferences communicated through subscriber behavior, especially as time passes. For example, if a subscriber says they are interested in hockey but begins buying baseball gear, then start mixing some baseball promotions into their emails.

As mentioned earlier, a major caveat to this is to be careful of giving much, if any, long-term weight to subscribers' browsing and purchase behavior during the holiday season.

Targeting

84

Send subscribers some segmented messages based on their expressed and implied preferences.

In addition to sending broadcast messages about broad topics to all your active subscribers, regularly use segmentation to send messages about a narrow topic only to those subscribers who are likely to respond. Using expressed and implied preferences to send emails targeted at groups of subscribers makes your emails more relevant, which increases in your open, click, and conversion rates, while reducing unsubscribes and spam complaints.

For instance, if you're opening a new store, segment your list by zip code and send a store-opening announcement to only your subscribers that live nearby. Segmenting by geography can also ensure that, for instance, all subscribers receive a promotion of winter gear at a time when their local temperatures start to cool.

In addition to geography and demographics, you can also segment by subscriber interest. For example, if you're promoting rock climbing gear, you could send the message to only those subscribers who have purchased that gear or browsed that product category in the past few months.

Targeting

85

Use dynamic content and personalization to add targeted content to emails.

Dynamic content and personalization can make even broadcast emails feel like one-to-one communications. These tools allow you to inject individual data and tailored content into emails, making them more personally relevant to recipients.

Historically, personalization focused largely on addressing an email recipient by name, but with the advent of Big Data, personalization has become much broader than that. You can now personalize subscribers' emails based on the following information:

- **Who they are**, including their name, where they work, what their birthday is, and other personal data points

- **Who they care about**, including information about their family members, friends, and work associates

- **What they did**, including browsing, purchases, physical activity, electricity usage, media consumption, and other behaviors

- **What others did in reaction**, including social media influence, the impact of the subscribers' reviews, and other actions taken

- **What they have**, including account and reward point balances, accessories for a purchased product, care or service instructions for a purchased product, and similar information
- **Where they are**, including local store information, local weather forecasts, geolocation-based messaging, and other location-based data

In all of these instances, it's now about demonstrating that you know a subscriber on a deeper level and can translate that knowledge into tailored content and deals.

An additional benefit of effective personalization is that it also gives email recipients confidence that the email they're reading is actually from you, and not from a phisher, who wouldn't have the knowledge you have.

Targeting & Personalization

86

When personalizing content, have a good default set up for when you don't have data for a particular subscriber.

If you're personalizing an email, you can end up with some pretty embarrassing results when you try to pull a data point and encounter a null set. Protect yourself from blank spaces, showing code, and other issues by establishing a default value for an attribute.

For example, if you're using first-name personalization in a subject line, set a default value of *Valued Customer* or something less corporate, such as *Deal-Seeker*, to avoid an awkward *Dear <$First_Name$>* or *Dear ,* in case you don't have a subscriber's name on record.

Additionally, depending on the size of the personalized content block, the default could be a call-to-action to supply the missing data point. For instance, your emails could highlight *Special Deals at Your Local Store*. Subscribers who have indicated a favorite store would see the deals, while those that haven't would see a call-to-action to *Tell us your favorite store to see these deals*.

Targeting & Personalization

87

Avoid misleading uses of personalization that suggest an email's content is deeply personalized when it is not.

Expectations are powerful. If you include a subscriber's name in a subject line, many subscribers will expect the content in the email to be tailored to them. If it isn't, some recipients will be disappointed.

For that reason, reserve first-name personalization in subject lines for segmented emails, emails that contain dynamic content or personal information, or emails sent directly in response to an action taken by a subscriber.

Similarly, in the body of an email, if you use language similar to *Recommendations for You* or *Just for You* and the content is generic, then you've trained your subscribers to pay less attention the next time you use that language.

Targeting & Personalization

88

Optimize the delivery time of your emails to increase their visibility in the inbox.

Although ISPs and third-party tool providers continue to roll out features that threaten the "last in, on top" inbox paradigm, there's still an advantage to timing the arrival of your email so that it's at the top of the recipient's inbox or promotional email folder.

Generally, the beginning of the work day (around 8 am), toward the end of the workday (around 4pm), and after dinner when the kids are in bed (around 8 pm) are times when engaging subscribers is easiest. Consider segmenting your list by time zone to target these periods more precisely.

However, as more and more emails are read on smartphones, these peak engagement periods are flattening out. Consider testing different send tactics for your mobile readers and desktop readers, or even tailoring send times to the behavior of individual subscribers.

You might also see a benefit in optimizing the day of the week that your emails are sent, although many brands find that decision is driven by promotions, store events, and other factors out of their control. Targeting different days of the month, especially those around common paydays like the 15th and last day of the month, can also be fruitful.

WORDS TO KNOW

triggered email
A message sent to an individual subscriber in response to an action taken by that person (e.g., cart abandoned) or because of the arrival of an event indicated by the subscriber (e.g., their birthday)

transactional email
A message sent to an individual subscriber in response to that person making a transaction, such as a purchase (e.g., order confirmation emails, shipping notification emails, etc.) or administrative request (e.g., password reset email, email address change confirmation email, etc.)

shopping cart abandonment email
A message sent to an individual subscriber in response to that person leaving one or more unpurchased items in their shopping cart

browse abandonment or browse retargeting email
A message sent to an individual subscriber in response to that person browsing certain pages of your website but not making a purchase

reengagement, reactivation, or win-back email
A message sent to an individual subscriber in response to that person having not engaged with your emails or made a purchase in a long time in an effort to get them to engage and make a purchase again

email automation
Triggered emails, personalization, dynamic content, and other tools that send emails or add

content to emails on a one-to-one or one-to-some basis without manual intervention according to rules established by a brand

opt up
When a subscriber opts into additional mailstreams from a brand via a preference center, loyalty program, sister brands, or another mechanism

Targeting & Personalization

89

Include promotional, seasonal, and service content in your transactional emails.

An order confirmation email can and should do more than just confirm that a customer successfully placed an order.

Transactional emails enjoy high open rates because they are expected and highly relevant to individual subscribers. Take advantage of that by including promotions and other content in your transactional emails that lead to more sales or improve customer satisfaction.

For example, if a customer buys a computer, you could promote accessories and software in the order confirmation email. Try to upsell buyers on accessories for the item they bought, on related or other affinity items, or on seasonal products.

That said, keep in mind that the main purpose of your transactional emails is to provide the customer with information about the transaction. To stay in compliance with CAN-SPAM's definition of a transactional email, place additional content below the transactional content or in a right-hand column. Also, limit the amount of promotional content to no more than a quarter of the overall email.

Targeting & Personalization

90

Address moments that matter by creating a variety of triggered emails that boost sales and improve customer service.

Triggered emails are among the highest performing emails you can send, regularly generating multifold more revenue per email than broadcast emails. They are super-effective because they are delivered at a time when subscribers are most receptive to their content.

The key is to identify moments that matter— the events that have a high impact on customer satisfaction, engagement, and purchase intent— and then use those events to trigger messaging that maximizes the positive impact.

Common events and the messages they can trigger include:

- **Making a purchase** >> Order confirmation email; shipping confirmation email; delivery confirmation email; activation or installation email; product review request email; short-supply and re-order emails; purchase anniversary email; service satisfaction survey email; upsell and cross-sell emails; other post-purchase emails

- **Registering at a website** >> Registration confirmation email

- **Registering for an event** >> Registration confirmation email, event countdown emails

- **Leaving an item in a shopping cart** >> Shopping cart abandonment email

- **Requesting to be notified when an item is back in stock** >> Back-in-stock notification email

- **Browsing product pages without buying** >> Browse abandonment email

- **Entering a contest or sweepstakes** >> Entry confirmation email, winner (or loser) notification email

- **Providing birth date of subscriber, spouse, children, or pets, or date of wedding anniversary** >> Birthday email, wedding anniversary email

- **Signing up to receive email, joined loyalty program** >> Welcome email, signup anniversary email

- **Not engaging with promotional emails** >> Reengagement, reactivation, or win-back email; re-permission email

Triggers that are less common would include mobile app inactivity, crossing a geofence, and the approach of potentially dangerous weather. And you can surely think up many other instances where a triggered email would help, educate, or reward your subscribers.

Although some triggered emails perform best when sent immediately following the trigger, some perform better when sent after a delay. Some triggered messages are more effective as a series of emails rather than a single one, and personalization can greatly improve the effectiveness of some triggered emails.

Targeting & Personalization

91

When using behavior triggers, be careful not to cannibalize natural behaviors.

Subscriber behavior is wonderful for powering targeted messages, but be mindful of not interrupting natural browsing and shopping behaviors.

For instance, abandoning shopping carts is a natural part of the shopping process for many consumers. Not every cart abandoner needs a cart abandonment email. Look at when the majority or a critical mass of customers return to their cart and check out on their own, and then set your cart abandonment email to launch shortly after that point. This way, you avoid sending emails to people who would have likely taken action without your email.

Also, consider setting a minimum shopping cart value to avoid triggering an email when there's very little revenue at stake. Similarly, if a lot of revenue is at stake, consider sending more than one email.

Targeting & Personalization

92

Be careful not to come across like Big Brother when using behavior triggers and personalization.

Some consumers are turned off by the idea that brands track their email and online activities. Be sensitive to these feelings by determining the right time to send each triggered email, recognizing that immediate triggers are not always the right answer. Additionally, when crafting your messaging, it's sometimes best to avoid mentioning explicitly that you noticed their behavior.

For instance, if you have a browse abandonment email that's triggered by subscribers that browse a big-ticket, high-consideration item like SLR cameras, you might be able to wait a day or two before sending that email. And the email itself might just highlight great camera options, a camera buying guide, or other helpful content without saying outright, *We noticed you looking at SLR cameras...*

Although some people will connect the dots, try to leave some doubt when you can. Make it seem plausible that the right content arriving at the right time is just a happy coincidence.

Targeting & Personalization

93

Avoid offering special incentives in messages triggered by a non-purchase.

Subscribers catch on very quickly. If you reward bad behavior, recipients will behave badly.

For instance, if you send an incentive when a shopper leaves an item in their shopping cart, they will abandon their carts every time and wait for the email incentive to arrive before purchasing. You will have trained your subscribers to delay their purchases and will have given margin away needlessly. It's now common behavior for many consumers to place items in their cart for consideration later—kind of like a wish list.

Rather than offering an incentive, just email a reminder of the item(s) in their cart. You can add urgency to these messages by mentioning sellout risks or highlighting the impending end of an existing sale. Depending on the product, you can also highlight reviews, educational material about the product category, or other informational content that might help the subscriber decide whether to purchase the product. These tactics are often enough to spur many subscribers to complete their purchase.

Save your triggered email incentives for when you really want to drive action, such as when you want to encourage a new subscriber to make their first purchase or win back a subscriber who hasn't made a purchase in a long time.

Targeting & Personalization

94

Place a cap on triggered email volume and establish a messaging hierarchy.

Triggered messages are one of the best ways to deliver more email to your most engaged subscribers. However, even the timeliest and most relevant emails can become excessive if too many messages arrive too often.

To keep this from happening, place a cap on how many triggered emails a subscriber can receive over the course of a day and limit how frequently a subscriber can receive the same triggered email.

For instance, if a subscriber browsed one product category and then another a few hours later, you probably shouldn't send them a browse abandonment email for each product category. You should pick one—probably the one for the more lucrative products.

Additionally, you shouldn't send the same browse abandonment email again if the subscriber returns and browses the same product category shortly thereafter—although you'll probably want to do some testing to find out what the best minimum interval is between browse abandonment emails.

In addition to caps, establish a message hierarchy to give priority to the most effective triggered emails. For instance, if a subscriber left an item in their shopping cart after browsing several items, you'd probably want to send a shopping cart abandonment email instead of a browse abandonment email.

Similarly, you might want to delay a product review request email if it was scheduled to go out on the same day as a birthday email to avoid having the two messages compete with each other.

Targeting & Personalization

95

Keep an inventory of your triggered email programs and regularly schedule time to update and fine-tune them.

Triggered emails are not "set it and forget it" programs. They are "review and renew" programs.

As your brand strategy evolves, copywriting can be honed, design can be polished, and targeting can be improved. Also, take advantage of opportunities to add seasonal content to triggered emails to make them more relevant.

Besides making improvements, checkups are necessary to prevent errors. ISP support for coding changes over time, so neglected triggered emails can breakdown and not render properly. Promotions change, links become outdated, logos are updated—all are good reasons to keep a close eye on your triggered email programs.

Quarterly reviews are a good idea. Reviews are also wise any time your email template or website is significantly updated.

Targeting

96

Use segmentation, triggered emails, and other tactics to send your most engaged subscribers more email.

Most of your email marketing revenue will be driven by a small percentage of your subscribers. Increase the opportunity presented by these high-value subscribers by sending them additional targeted messages by using segmentation, setting up triggered emails that respond as they engage, and presenting them with opportunities to opt up into additional mailstreams.

Those other mailstreams could be for a loyalty program, offers from sister brands, or ones on other topics selected by the subscriber. When trying to secure these additional opt-ins, don't forget to make the signups as simple as possible and to explain what's in it for the subscriber.

Inactivity

*"That email you're going to send next week?
If you didn't send it, how many people would
complain and wonder where it is? Because if
they're not complaining when you don't show up,
then you don't really have permission."*
—Seth Godin, Author of *Permission Marketing*
and many other books

Sometimes subscribers aren't interested in your emails anymore but don't unsubscribe for some reason. Subscribers who haven't engaged with your emails in a long time represent a shrinking revenue opportunity and growing risk to your ability to get your emails delivered. They also dampen your performance metrics, making it more difficult to see positive changes.

It's worth trying to get these subscribers engaged with your emails again, but realistically you'll end up letting most of them go.

WORDS TO KNOW

inactivity
When a subscriber has not opened or clicked in any of your emails in a long time

post-click metrics
Browsing, carting, and other activities on your site that take place after someone clicks through one of your emails

click-to-open rate
Percentage of subscribers who opened an email that also clicked the content inside, which is calculated by dividing clicks by opens

unique opens
The number of subscribers who loaded or rendered the images of an email at least once; a method of measuring opens that only counts the first open made by individual subscribers, ignoring any subsequent opens

total opens
The number of times the images of an email were loaded or rendered; a method of measuring opens that includes repeat opens by an individual subscriber

unique clicks
The number of subscribers who selected a link or linked image in an email at least once and visited the associated landing page; a method of measuring clicks that only counts the first click made by individual subscribers, ignoring any subsequent clicks

total clicks
The number of times the links or linked images in an email were selected by subscribers, who then

visited the associated landing page; a method of measuring clicks that includes repeat clicks by an individual subscriber

reengage or reactivate
Getting a subscriber to open or click one of your emails after a long period of having not done so

re-permission email
A message that asks a subscriber to reconfirm their subscription by clicking a link in the email in order to remain on your active mailing list

Inactivity

97

Define inactive subscribers by their email behaviors, but also consider their customer behaviors.

Defining inactivity is a thorny issue because business owners, ISPs, and email marketers each have their own definition of *inactive* that's geared toward their own key constituent.

Business owners are focused on customers. They mostly care about whether emails are directly generating revenue or profits or are indirectly influencing sales by leading to post-click activities like browsing and carting.

They care a lot about whether a subscriber is an active customer. Many believe that being an active customer trumps being an inactive subscriber—especially if they understand the unseen influence that unopened and unclicked emails can have on subscribers.

ISPs, on the other hand, are focused on their email users. They don't care if one of their users is one of your best customers. They only care if that user is engaging with your emails by opening them, scrolling through them, clicking in them, forwarding them, and taking other positive actions—many of which are only visible to ISPs.

Email Marketers Have 2 Masters, 2 Sets of Success Metrics

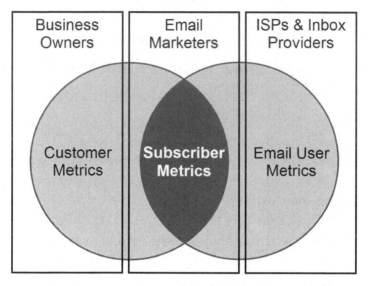

FIGURE 4

If your subscriber hasn't done any of those in a long while, ISPs will start to junk or block your emails to that user. And if they see that too many of their users haven't engaged with your emails in a long time, they will begin junking or blocking all of your emails.

Occupying the space between business owners and ISPs, email marketers are focused on their subscribers. (See Fig. 4.) They need to care about business metrics like conversions and the subscriber's activity in other channels. However, they also need to care about email metrics like click-to-open rates and total and unique opens and clicks, as those measure list health and subscriber progression down the sales funnel.

When making decisions about subscriber inactivity, email marketers need to find the middle ground between the concerns that business owners have about customer metrics and the concerns that ISPs have about email user metrics.

The best definition of an inactive subscriber lies at the intersection of those two vantage points— namely, a heavy focus on lack of opens and clicks, while being mindful of whether the subscriber is one of your better customers.

Because of image blocking and the ability of the subject lines of unopened emails to drive action, opens and clicks might not accurately reflect a subscriber's engagement. For that reason, you might want to accelerate the reengagement of and delay the re-permissioning of inactive subscribers whom you know to be valuable active customers.

Even then, you can't delay re-permissioning forever, as deliverability risks continue to mount the longer a subscriber is inactive.

Inactivity

98

Send your inactive subscribers different messaging at a lower frequency.

Once a subscriber has been inactive for many months, the chance of them becoming active again is small but definitely worth pursuing.

To try to reengage inactive subscribers, send them different emails than you send the rest of your list. Send win-back emails touting your richest offers, and consider using different subject lines and different dynamic content in your broadcast emails that go to actives. *We miss you* is a common subject line phrase for win-back emails.

Also, consider sending non-promotional content, such as requests for them to update their email preferences or to complete a survey, which might give you information you can use to send them targeted email. Gaining additional insights that you can use for targeting is key because otherwise they're likely to go inactive again.

Sometimes withholding emails from inactives for a period of weeks can be effective, too, because some of them will notice the absence of your emails and then respond when you start sending again.

Because ISPs use engagement metrics in their

filtering algorithms, having lots of inactive subscribers poses a risk to your deliverability. Reduce that risk by emailing inactives considerably less frequently. For instance, if you send daily emails, reduce that to weekly for inactives. Or if you send weekly emails, reduce that to once per month.

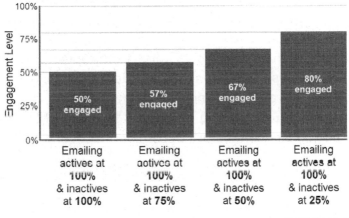

Increasing Engagement by Mailing Inactives Less Often

For an email list that's 50% active subscribers and 50% inactive subscribers

FIGURE 5

Doing so can have a dramatic effect on how engaged your subscribers look in the eyes of ISPs. Generally, if 30% to 50% of your list is inactive, reducing your mailings to inactive subscribers by 75% can increase the engagement level profile of your sends by 30% to 60%. (See Fig. 5.)

In addition to protecting your deliverability, less frequent mailings to inactives can cause some of them to actually pay more attention to your emails and reengage.

In addition to trying to reengage inactive subscribers, if your email data can identify subscribers who are likely to become inactive, you can preemptively treat those subscribers differently, too, in an effort to keep them active. In other words, feel free to intervene with triggered messaging, dynamic content, and other tactics before a subscriber technically becomes inactive.

If you have the data and capabilities, you might also consider reaching out to inactive subscribers via other channels, such as direct mail, SMS, and targeted display ads online, in order to reactivate them. This approach might be particularly warranted for reaching customers who were high-value subscribers before becoming inactive.

Inactivity

99

Send a series of re-permission emails before you remove a chronically inactive subscriber from your email list.

If your reactivation efforts fail, then it's time to work toward removing a chronically inactive subscriber. However, don't just remove a subscriber from your list without warning.

Send a series of re-permission emails asking the subscriber to indicate either *Yes, I'd like to continue receiving special offers* or *No, please unsubscribe me*—or language along those lines.

Send up to three re-permission emails. Use different subject lines and send them on different days and at different times of the day to increase the response rate.

A *Yes* click in any of these emails puts the subscriber back on your active email list, as this action reconfirms their subscription. Selecting *No* should take them to your preference center or opt-out page. And if the subscriber doesn't respond to any of the re-permission emails, then you should unsubscribe them.

Response rates for re-permission emails tend to

be very low, but they are worth the effort. Setting up an automated program to send these triggered emails takes relatively little work after you've set up a program to recognize chronically inactive subscribers.

Additionally, subscribers lost due to inactivity may react positively to your courteous efforts if they discover the re-permission emails later.

Landing Pages

"When you neglect the landing page, the money you spend on acquisition and retention is largely wasted, flushed down the proverbial toilet."

—Tim Ash, Maura Ginty, and Rich Page, Coauthors of *Landing Page Optimization*

The landing page is the final stage of email interaction. Until subscribers are able to perform a wide range of transactions entirely within an email, landing pages will be vital to completing the conversation started by an email.

WORDS TO KNOW

landing page
Webpage, app, and any other destination that subscribers are directed to when they click a call-to-action in one of your emails

Landing Pages

100

Design your landing pages so they look good and function well across a wide range of platforms and devices.

Just as emails must display well on a variety of email clients and devices, landing pages must also perform well in a variety of environments.

For instance, having a mobile-friendly email design is considerably less effective if subscribers have to click through to a website that's not optimized for mobile. Subscribers should have a consistent, user-friendly experience when they move from an email to a landing page.

Landing Pages

101

Use language and images from the email on the landing page to create a smooth transition from email to landing page.

Give subscribers visual reassurances that they arrived on the right landing page after clicking through an email by using some of the same language, images, and other design elements.

Doing so creates continuity between the email and the landing page that's comforting to subscribers. Those who are unsure whether they've arrived at the right page might abandon your site or feel less certain about converting.

Landing Pages

102

Use landing pages that minimize the number of clicks it takes for subscribers to convert.

Every extra click you require a customer to make increases the chance that the customer will abandon your site, so take subscribers directly to the content they're expecting when they click through your email.

For example, if they click a banner promoting your clearance products in your email, don't direct a subscriber to your homepage, even if there's a banner on your homepage promoting the clearance selection.

Too often, homepages are used as landing pages when a product category, product page, blog post, or another page would save the subscriber a click or two. Even site search results pages can serve as very versatile landing pages.

Also consider creating custom landing pages when there's no natural existing landing page for an email's call-to-action.

Landing Pages

103

Don't make subscribers hunt for the items featured in your emails.

If you use a product image in an email to promote a product category, position that featured product prominently on the landing page. Don't make subscribers scroll through page after page of products to find the one you featured.

If you can't reposition the product on the landing page, consider providing a link to the item's product page in the email—or at least include a caption in the email that includes the brand or name of the item so subscribers can search for it on your site.

Additionally, if you don't carry all the items in an image provided by the manufacturer, don't use the image. It erodes trust and frustrates subscribers when they can't find an item that you signaled you carried.

Landing Pages

104

Design well-branded landing pages and email administration pages that offer a clear path forward.

Imagine you're walking through a store and see signs for a demonstration of a product you're interested in. You follow the signs to the back of the store and through a door that leads into the back alley, where you see the product demonstration going on. It's not the best brand impression, so chances are you're not going to stick around.

This same scenario plays out in email programs when subscribers are directed to barren pages with no branding, no navigation, and no path forward. I call it *back alley syndrome*, and it's most prevalent on pages that confirm an opt-out, a preference change, an email signup, and other administrative functions. But it also occurs on email landing pages for videos, surveys, and other special, one-off content.

Often these are the result of templates provided by ESPs and other vendors. In most cases, you can customize these pages to offer a better experience.

Dead-end pages prematurely end brand interactions and make bad impressions. Always offer a path forward for subscribers.

Landing Pages

105

Don't remove a landing page too quickly without providing an alternative.

Some subscribers will click through an email days or even weeks after receiving it, so removing email landing pages when a product sells out or a sale ends can generate *404 page not found* errors for subscribers. That frustrates and confuses subscribers, who might be unsure whether they've arrived at the right page or if a product is still available, and it fails to capitalize on their interest.

For product pages, if you plan on restocking the item, keep the page live. Consider offering visitors the option to sign up to receive a back-in-stock email notification when the item is available again. If the product was one-of-a-kind, consider redirecting visitors to similar items, while also notifying them that the item they originally sought has sold.

For sale event pages, consider redirecting visitors to a current sale page or posting a message that the sale has ended and suggesting other pages for them to visit.

Quality Assurance & Disaster Planning

"You shouldn't worry about when you will make an error. Instead, you should feel confident that you will be able to handle it when it happens to you."

—Jeanniey Mullen and David Daniels, Coauthors of *Email Marketing an Hour a Day*

Making mistakes in a channel that's high volume, high reach, and lightning fast is easy. In fact, it's practically inevitable. Therefore, in addition to putting checks in place to minimize the chance of error, prepare a disaster response plan.

WORDS TO KNOW

quality assurance
Ensuring that email content is error-free and functions properly and that the intended subscribers receive that content at the intended time

apology email
A message sent in response to an error or mishap

Quality Assurance & Disaster Planning

106

Create a pre-send checklist
to reduce the possibility of making
a serious mistake.

The most common email errors involve incorrect subject lines, typos, broken personalization, misdirected links, and deployment mishaps like sending the same email twice or sending an email to the wrong segment.

To reduce mistakes, use the following checklist as a starting point for your own:

☐ Do you have the right content scheduled for the right date? Double-check sends that are based on holidays whose dates change from year to year, such as Thanksgiving and Easter. And read the content one last time to look for errors.

☐ Do you have the right list? That's vital if you are segmenting the email, running a test on a portion of your list, or operating multiple brands.

☐ Do you have the right personalization? Check the logic and assets for your personalization and dynamic content.

☐ Do you have the right sender name? This is particularly critical if you operate multiple brands.

☐ Do you have the right subject line? Avoid using placeholder text and don't leave subject line writing until the last moment.

☐ Do you have the right rendering? Use a rendering preview tool or view a test send in all the major email client and browser combinations to make sure the message displays as intended.

☐ Do you have the right landing pages? Do all the links in the email lead to the correct pages, especially those for the key calls-to-action?

If content or other mistakes are routinely made, examine your production process to identify practices that invite errors and then set up additional safeguards.

Quality Assurance & Disaster Planning

107

Don't draw undue attention to email mistakes by overreacting.

Very few email errors are serious enough to need correcting. Most are trivial and merely embarrassing, such as:

- Typos
- Image formatting and rendering issues
- One minor broken link among many
- Temporary issues such as an image server going down for a short period
- Broken personalization
- Minor deployment mistakes such as sending an email earlier than intended or sending it twice

Small errors are likely to go unnoticed or understood as errors if they are noticed. It's often better to move on.

That said, issues that are more serious are worth addressing.

Quality Assurance & Disaster Planning

108

Take steps to reduce the impact of email marketing mistakes when they are discovered quickly.

When you discover a moderate to serious mistake in the content, links, targeting, or timing of an email that you've just sent, you can take a number of actions to limit the damage it causes.

First, stop the send if it hasn't completed. If your list is really large, a send could take hours, so you might have time to halt it and fix the error before resuming the send. That way, fewer subscribers are exposed to the error.

Second, you can fix some content errors post-send. For instance, if the mistake is in an image, correct it and then replace the hosted source file with the corrected image. If the mistake is with a link, see whether you can get the link redirected to the correct page.

Third, if the email contains incorrect information, use the landing page for the email to clarify the offer, timing of the event, or other details.

And finally, consider using social media and other channels to address any confusion caused by an email by emphasizing the correct information.

Along the way, check your email analytics to

try to determine how large an impact the error is having. Sometimes things aren't as bad as you think, which might influence how you proceed with damage control measures.

Quality Assurance & Disaster Planning

109

Have an apology email drafted but only send it, or resend an email, in the case of a very serious error.

Most brands don't send a single apology email over the course of a year. And most of the apology emails that are sent are not in response to email errors, but rather site outages and other events. So to say that apology emails are rare is a colossal understatement.

However, you want to be prepared in the event that misfortune befalls you, so have a process in place so you can respond quickly. To that end, have an apology email drafted that can be quickly updated with the necessary information.

This same email could also be used to get information out quickly to subscribers concerning events likely to have an impact on them and your operations, such as a major storm or other natural disaster.

Serious errors come in a few different varieties, each of which deserves a different response. First, for significant errors that only affect a small portion of your email subscribers, consider sending an apology email or a resend of the original email with a message of explanation at the top that's segmented only to those affected.

For instance, if you send subscribers personalized discount codes and your website wasn't set up properly to accept those codes at the time of the send, then you could send an apology email to just those subscribers who tried to use their codes, telling them that the issue has been fixed and to please try again.

Second, for a serious mistake that only affects your email subscribers, an apology is necessary to clear things up and mend the relationship. A good example of this kind of mistake would be a company that owns or services multiple brands accidently sending a message intended for the subscribers of one brand to the subscribers of another brand.

Permission is sacred. Accidently violating it is worth apologizing for and making it clear to subscribers that they won't receive any more messages from the brand—with the subtext being, "Please don't mark that email as spam."

And third, for particularly harmful or hurtful email mistakes—especially if a significant number of people are talking about it on social media—an apology email should be part of a full-spectrum apology that includes reaching out via social media and making statements to the media.

One last tip: If you send an apology email or resend an email, make certain that it is perfect. You don't want to follow one mistake with another.

Unsubscribe Process

"Requiring subscribers to jump through hoops to be removed from your mailing list will either result in them clicking the Report Spam button instead or finishing the process but leaving with a negative opinion of your company or brand."

—Simms Jenkins, Author of *The Truth about Email Marketing*

Marketers tend to think of unsubscribes in very negative terms, but this negativity should be saved for spam complaints, which are an unequivocal form of failure. If a subscriber wants to leave your list, you'd much prefer they unsubscribe than resort to complaining.

First and foremost, unsubscribes don't hurt your sender reputation, unlike spam complaints. Second, if recipients unsubscribe, it indicates that they trust you to honor their opt-out, which is a positive sign from a brand perspective. Third, if they click the unsubscribe link, you have an opportunity to potentially address the reason they're opting out or direct them to your other marketing channels, such as social media. And finally, you also have a chance to honor their opt-out gracefully and have the last word, which should be one of thanks.

WORDS TO KNOW

opt-out process
How subscribers remove themselves from your mailing list

list churn
Subscribers lost to unsubscribes, spam complaints, and bounces from email addresses that no longer work

unsubscribe page
Webpage that is launched when subscribers click the unsubscribe link in your emails where subscribers complete the unsubscribe process

opt down
When a subscriber chooses to receive a brand's emails less frequently

opt over
When a subscriber opts into one of your other channels, such as social or mobile, during your email unsubscribe process

Unsubscribe Process

110

Recognize that list growth can also be boosted by reducing unsubscribes.

To grow your list on an absolute basis, the number of new subscribers that you add during a period of time has to exceed your list churn—that is, subscribers lost to unsubscribes, spam complaints, and hard bounces from email addresses that no longer work.

With most brands losing 25% or more of their subscribers each year, list churn is a significant drag on list growth. Developing strategies to reduce unsubscribes, as well as spam complaints, should be part of your list growth plans.

Unsubscribe Process

111

Clearly identify the subscriber on the opt-out page and in the preference center.

Give the subscriber assurances that they've arrived at their opt-out page or preference center by showing at least their email address prominently, if not other information, such as their name.

Doing this also helps to prevent recipients of a forwarded email from unintentionally opting out a subscriber.

Unsubscribe Process

112

Give subscribers options in addition to completely opting out.

You absolutely don't want to impede a subscriber from opting out, but recognize that you might be able to address the issue that's driving them to unsubscribe.

A common reason subscribers opt out is that they feel they get too many emails from the sender. Providing the ability to opt-down and receive fewer emails can retain some subscribers who feel this way. Once a month and once a week are common opt-down email frequency choices.

Another reason subscribers give for opting out is that the emails were not relevant. Letting subscribers select or change content or product preferences can correct that problem.

Some subscribers simply want to change their email address and think they need to unsubscribe and then re-subscribe. Providing a *Change Your Email Address* link in your emails, and a similar option in your preference center or on your unsubscribe page, simplifies this process and eliminates the risk that they never get around to re-subscribing after opting out.

This option also keeps your customer and subscriber records clean by ensuring that you attribute both the subscriber's old and new email address to a single customer file, rather than mistakenly attributing the two addresses to two customers.

Other subscribers might still want to receive messages from you but would prefer to get them via another channel. You might be losing an email subscriber, but if you give them the ability to opt over to direct mail, a social network, or some other touchpoint, you'll keep the lines of communication open with the customer, which should be a business priority.

If you have sister brands, giving outgoing subscribers the option to sign up for emails from those brands might also pay off.

During the holiday season, when email volume spikes, you might also consider giving subscribers the option to pause or "snooze" their subscription until after Christmas or the New Year.

And lastly, when given the option to *Stay Subscribed*, a surprising number of subscribers do so, which indicates that some are just exploring their options. Remind subscribers of the benefits of receiving your emails and give them the chance to re-affirm their subscription.

Unsubscribe Process

113

Be gracious when subscribers opt out to avoid brand damage.

Just because a subscriber doesn't want to receive any more emails from you doesn't necessarily mean they won't buy from you again or interact with you via other channels. So be polite and gracious for the sake of your brand relationship, if not for the sake of your email relationship.

For instance, say you're sorry to see them go and hope that they'll re-subscribe in the future. If your business is a restaurant, thank the patron for being a subscriber and say you hope to see them in one of your restaurants soon. If you're running a nonprofit, reiterate the importance of your mission and show your appreciation of the subscriber's support.

Whatever you do, don't act as if the relationship is over, because it most likely isn't. And even if the relationship is over for the moment, nothing is permanent.

Unsubscribe Process

114

Confirm an unsubscribe request via the channel through which it was requested.

Most unsubscribe requests will occur your website when a subscriber clicks the unsubscribe link in one of your emails and arrives at your unsubscribe page or preference center. Confirm those opt-outs on your website. Sending an email confirming that a subscriber opted out might irritate them—perhaps to the point that they hit the Report Spam button.

The negative risks associated with these emails usually outweigh any benefits, such as helping protect against the rare cases of malicious opt-outs, when a person uses your opt-out page to unsubscribe someone else, or cases of recipients of a forwarded email unintentionally opting out a subscriber.

One exception to this is if the subscriber is paying to receive the emails or paying for a service that operates primarily through the emails. In that case, an opt-out confirmation email is wise because it's more of a termination-of-service notification in these cases.

Also, if you allow subscribers to opt-out by replying to one of your emails with *unsubscribe* or some other word in the subject line, then sending those people an opt-out confirmation email is completely appropriate.

Unsubscribe requests that come through your call center can be verbally confirmed on the spot, and requests that come through the mail should be confirmed in a letter.

Unsubscribe Process

115

Routinely audit your opt-out processes to make sure they are working properly.

Consumers expect you to honor unsubscribe requests immediately and often report any additional emails they receive afterward as spam. CAN-SPAM also requires that you honor unsubscribe requests swiftly, so taking care of opt-outs is a matter of quality assurance, good customer service, and legal responsibility.

Even if you use an email service provider to handle opt-outs through the unsubscribe link in your emails, periodically check and make sure they're working as expected. However, you should put more emphasis on checking other opt-out pathways, such as opt-outs via email replies, via call center calls, and via postal mail.

Testing

"For marketers, testing is at the heart of improving conversion, measuring is at the heart of holding these conversion improvements to an increasing standard, and optimization is at the heart of persuasion."
—Bryan Eisenberg, Author of *Always Be Testing*

A vigorous testing program is the hallmark of a great email program. It is a critical form of listening and helps your program to be more user-friendly. Testing different subject lines, email designs, offers, content, and landing pages helps you to understand what motivates, interests, and appeals to your subscribers, so you can serve them better.

Testing should also be inspired by intriguing case studies you read and cool email designs or tactics you encounter. Every brand has a different image, voice, and audience, so testing is necessary to see if you can translate tactics and strategies used by other brands into success for your brand.

Although uncovering huge performance differences is rare, keep in mind that small improvements add up to big results over time.

WORDS TO KNOW

A/B testing
Exposing a portion of your subscribers to one version of an email or landing page and another portion of your subscribers to another version and seeing which version performs better

statistically relevant
Having enough data from a test that the results are meaningful rather than simply the result of chance

50/50 split test
Exposing half your subscribers to one version of an email or landing page and the other half of your subscribers to another version and seeing which version performs better to inform future decisions

10/10/80 split test
Exposing 10% of your subscribers to one version of an email or landing page and another 10% of your subscribers to another version, seeing which version performs better, and then exposing the remaining 80% of your subscribers to that winning version

multivariate testing
Similar to A/B testing, except multiple variations in an email or landing page are tested simultaneously, which requires lots of data to do accurately

champion
During an A/B test, your existing design or process

challenger
During an A/B test, the design or process that you think will be an improvement to your existing design or process

---

Testing

116

Use your email metrics to identify areas for improvement and future testing.

The results of your email campaigns will help you understand what's working and what's not, and can inform your decisions about what to test.

For instance, if for a particular campaign, your open rate was around your average but your click rate was below average, then it would indicate that the content of your email wasn't compelling enough.

If your click rate was about average but your conversion rate was below average, either the email content set the wrong expectations or there are problems on the landing pages for that email. Perhaps the messaging on the landing page wasn't compelling enough, or perhaps the landing page didn't provide a smooth transition from the email, causing subscribers to believe they arrived at the wrong page and then abandon your site.

If your click-to-open rate is low—that is, a high open rate with a low click rate—then it would indicate a disconnect between the expectations set by your subject line and the content of the email.

If you wanted recipients to share your message but your total opens was nearly identical to your unique opens, then subscribers didn't find the content worth sharing—at least not by forwarding the email.

Mapping your click-to-open rate across the various calls-to-action within your email can tell you which CTAs subscribers found most compelling. It can also give you insights into how far subscribers were scrolling, which might inform future positioning of content.

That's just a sampling of the ways your email metrics can direct you toward tests that are more likely to yield actionable insights.

Testing

117

Create a calendar or list of tests to run so you can methodically build on your findings.

Take the time to plan your testing to ensure that you're not only focusing your efforts on the pain points where you have the most to gain, but also that you are backing up your challenger with a solid hypothesis. Also, use your calendar to help build on what you learned from previous tests.

Analytics, customer surveys, diary studies, and focus groups can help you identify which elements of your email program are most in need of testing and give you ideas for challenger designs and processes.

Pretty much everything is open to testing, but here are some common A/B tests to get you started:

Email Design
Subject lines
☐ Different lengths
☐ Number of components (e.g., highlighting one offer vs. two)
☐ Different offers (e.g., percent vs. dollar discount)
☐ Statement vs. question

☐ Value vs. lifestyle appeal

☐ First-name personalization vs. generic address or none

☐ Different capitalization, punctuation, and special characters

Headline

☐ Different wording

☐ Different lengths

☐ Different sizes

☐ Different fonts or styling

Images

☐ Different sizes

☐ Different position

☐ Model vs. product

☐ Positioning of model (e.g., looking straight vs. looking toward key copy or call-to-action vs. looking away from it)

☐ Live shot vs. illustration

☐ Static image vs. animation vs. video

☐ Manufacturer image vs. your image vs. customer image

Copy

☐ Different position relative to images

☐ Different copy lengths

☐ Different benefits or features highlighted

☐ Promotional vs. non-promotional copy

☐ Different social proof (e.g., testimonials) vs. none

Calls-to-action

- ☐ Different sizes
- ☐ Button vs. link
- ☐ Different button shape
- ☐ Different wording
- ☐ Different colors
- ☐ Different positions
- ☐ Different landing pages
- ☐ High commitment vs. low commitment (e.g., *Buy Now* vs. *Learn More*)

Product grid

- ☐ Number of columns in grid (e.g., two vs. three)
- ☐ Which product elements to include (e.g. product name, brand, price, etc.)

Secondary messages

- ☐ Number of secondary messages, including none
- ☐ Order of secondary messages
- ☐ Related to primary message vs. not

Processes

Subscription process

- ☐ Different signup language
- ☐ Different form elements (e.g., just email address vs. more fields)
- ☐ Making fields optional vs. required
- ☐ Showing or linking to sample emails vs. not

Triggered messages

- ☐ How quickly to send the message after it's triggered
- ☐ Whether to send a series of triggered emails and how many to send

Inactivity

- ☐ Different lengths of inactivity
- ☐ Different content tactics to reengage (e.g., rich offer, different subject lines, etc.)
- ☐ Different re-permission messaging

Unsubscribe process

- ☐ Different language on opt-out page
- ☐ Different alternatives made available

Testing

118

Perform tests on groups of active, unbiased subscribers.

Choosing a poor sample of subscribers for your A/B tests can significantly skew the results, making them potentially unreliable.

First, make sure you perform tests with active subscribers. Including inactive subscribers in your testing sample weakens results, in addition to directing your focus away from the subscribers who are driving the performance of your email program.

Of course, the one exception to this is if your testing is specifically aimed at inactives, such as a test of win-back messaging.

And second, when testing email design changes, choose sample groups composed of new subscribers. Existing subscribers will likely resist design changes initially and it can take a while to change their expectations and retrain how they interact with your emails. New subscribers aren't biased by interactions with your previous designs, so they are the ideal candidates for these tests.

Testing

119

Make sure the results of your email tests are statistically significant.

If your test groups are too small, then the results will generally not be reliable. So use large, randomized groups—of, say, several thousand active subscribers—and aim for at least 150 conversions for each variation. Doing so ensures that the results are statistically significant.

Whether results are statistically significant is measured in terms of confidence. Your goal is to reach 95% confidence that the results didn't happen by chance before calling the test complete.

Email service providers often provide at least simple testing functionality that includes confidence measures. If not, testing tool providers exist.

In regards to email testing, if your email list is small, then you'll likely be able to do only 50/50 split tests. That's where you send one version of an email to half your list and another version to the other half of your list. You then see which version performs better and use the learnings from the test to inform future email content and design decisions.

If your email list is large, you might be able to do 10/10/80 split tests. That's where you create two versions of an email, send each version to

10% of your list, and then later send the winning version to the remaining 80% of your list.

With 50/50 and 10/10/80 splits, it's often best to have only one variation between the two versions that you send so that it's clear what exactly is responsible for the difference in response. For instance, the two versions of an email would be exactly the same except that one would have a red CTA button and the other a blue button. That way, if the email with the red button performs better, you know it's because of the button color, which would inform your future design decisions.

If your email list is truly huge, you might be able to do multivariate testing, where multiple variations in an email are tested simultaneously. This flavor of A/B testing is trickier to set up and requires a lot of data to get meaningful results, but the advantage is that you get better information about how each of the variations interact with each another. That data can help you identify the variations that have the most impact on your goal.

Similar math would apply to the testing of landing pages, signup forms, preference centers, unsubscribe pages, and other email-related webpages.

Be prepared for some—perhaps many—of your tests to be inconclusive because the difference in performance between the two versions is small. You'll also uncover some hidden gems, however, where the performance difference is 25%, 50%, or even more than 100%.

As a reminder, make sure that you're using the appropriate success metrics for your test. Focus on the metrics that really matter, such as clicks and conversions, even when judging subject lines and other elements early in an email interaction.

Testing

120

Challenge your new champions in order to verify gains and uncover new gains.

Finding a new champion doesn't mean your testing is complete. Sometimes the improvements from a change are fleeting because they're driven by novelty, so it's important to re-test the same element or process periodically to reconfirm the results or to uncover additional improvements.

Also, keep in mind changes in production and technology costs as they can have a significant effect on calculations. For instance, a drastic drop in production costs associated with a tactic can turn it from a failed challenger into a new champion.

The Last Word on Practice Guidelines

The Tested Rule

Because brands and their subscribers are different and sometimes face unique circumstances, there are instances where selectively, temporarily, or permanently bending or breaking the Practice Guidelines will be advantageous.

Recognizing that gives us our second Power Rule, *The Tested Rule:*

Break the rules, but only if you can prove that doing so leads to superior long-term performance.

Don't break the rules just to break the rules. Do so with purpose and with a full realization of the potential benefits and risks.

It's not difficult to find celebrated anomalies of brands breaking the rules successfully, but you won't find many because usually the results just aren't that impressive. Moreover, you'll rarely hear about all the brands that broke the rules and lost.

PART II

The Interconnections

Having broken email marketing down into individual components, let's now put the pieces back together so you can see how different groups of components function as one.

Understanding the following concepts allows you to coordinate your efforts, work toward a particular goal, and create an effective, cohesive experience for your subscribers.

An Integrated View of

The Subscriber Lifecycle

"The customers are the assets; not the store and not the ecommerce sites."

—Michael Brown, Partner at A.T. Kearney

To maximize the value of an email relationship, you need to cater to your subscribers' needs and wants throughout their entire subscriber lifecycle— from the time they sign up to the time they unsubscribe. To do that, you have to develop tactics that address the major subscriber moments from beginning to end.

The subscriber lifecycle has 6 stages: Acquisition, Onboarding, Engagement, Reengagement, Super-Engagement, and Transition.

The acquisition and onboarding stages are at the start of the email relationship. The three engagement stages are in the middle. And the transition stage is at the end of the lifecycle. (See Fig. 6.) Many brands don't have programs in place to address subscribers during each of these stages, but every brand should.

The Subscriber Lifecycle

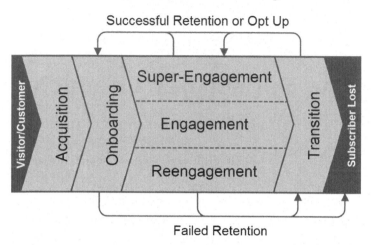

FIGURE 6

The **acquisition stage** consists of the methods you use to get consumers to opt in to your email program, as well as the entirety of a confirmed opt-in process (Rule 25). This is where you answer the *What's in it for me?* question would-be subscribers are asking themselves (Rules 31 & 38) and where you set content and frequency expectations (Rule 34).

Depending on the acquisition source, consumers will need a different level of convincing and of explanation, just as the level of permission should be higher for sources far from your sales and service operations (Rule 28).

The **onboarding stage** consists of your opt-in confirmation page and your welcome email or welcome email series. This stage starts immediately after the acquisition stage (Rules 41 & 42) and could last many weeks (Rule 43).

Again, you'll want to address new subscribers differently depending on their acquisition source and customer history (Rule 44).

The *engagement stage* consists of your baseline promotional mailstream. For most brands, these will be your regularly scheduled broadcast emails, plus seasonal fluctuations in frequency (Rule 80).

Supplementing or replacing the engagement stage, the *reengagement stage* consists of messaging tactics designed to address subscribers who are inactive or are in danger of soon becoming inactive. These tactics include:

- Sending win-back, reengagement, or reactivation emails

- Sending different messages or using different envelope or body content than what engaged subscribers receive

- Withholding emails for a number of weeks

- Drastically reducing email frequency to minimize the risk to your sender reputation posed by inactive subscribers (Rule 98)

The purpose of the reengagement stage is to return disengaged subscribers to the engagement stage rather than having them progress to the transition stage.

Supplementing or replacing the engagement stage, the *super-engagement stage* consists of messaging tactics that further engage subscribers who are already highly engaged. These tactics, all of which result in these subscribers receiving additional emails, include:

- Setting up an array of triggered messages, including browse and cart abandonment emails, back-in-stock notification emails, post-purchase emails, and replenishment emails (Rule 90)

- Sending segmented messages (Rule 84) based on browse and purchase behavior, expressed preferences, and progressive profiling (Rules 35 & 83)

- Giving subscribers opportunities to give you more information through your preference center and progressive profiling and then using that information to power segmentation and personalization (Rule 63)

- Offering a loyalty program with a supplemental mailstream or a higher-volume mailstream that replaces the one that non-loyalty members receive

- Getting subscribers to opt up into additional mailstreams, whether offered by your brand or by your sister brands (Rule 96)

While reengagement reduces the risks posed by inactives, super-engagement fosters more opportunities with active subscribers.

And lastly, the *transition stage* consists of your unsubscribe page, preference center, opt-out confirmation page, and re-permission emails (Rule

99). The purpose of the transition stage is two-fold.

First, you want to avoid unnecessary damage to your sender reputation. Making it very easy for subscribers to withdraw their permission helps you minimizing spam complaints (Rule 5), and letting go of chronically inactive subscribers increases the engagement level of your subscriber base (Rule 6).

And second, you want to attempt to retain the subscriber by giving them options other than opting out, such as reducing the frequency at which they receive messages or changing their content preferences so the emails they receive are more relevant. In the best possible scenario, a subscriber might adjust their preferences and suddenly be super-engaged. But if none of that can be achieved, then you want to get them to opt over to another channel that will serve them better and lessen the loss of them as an email subscriber (Rule 112).

Always keep in mind that an unsubscribe might not be the permanent end of an email relationship.

People do re-subscribe occasionally through a different email address. And even more importantly, the end of an email relationship doesn't mean the end of a business relationship. So be courteous and gracious during the unsubscribe process to avoid brand damage (Rule

113). Your customers' experiences with your email program are just one facet of their overall impression of your brand.

Although subscribers generally progress though each stage of the lifecycle in a linear fashion—moving from acquisition to onboarding to engagement and finally to transition—that won't always be the case. Depending on what your email program offers, there could be opportunities at each stage to move back to another stage.

For instance, during the transition stage, a subscriber could opt out of the mailstream they were in and then opt into a new one, putting them back at the onboarding stage with the new mailstream. And during the reengagement stage, an email asking the subscriber to update their preferences could lead to the same change of mailstream.

Of course, there are always opportunities for subscribers to skip ahead as well, usually resulting in the abrupt end of the email relationship. For instance, a subscriber could opt-out during onboarding, skipping right to the transition stage. And during the engagement stages, they could report your emails as spam or your emails to them could hard bounce, meaning an immediate loss of the subscriber.

So, just as a subscriber can move up and down through the three engagement stages, they might also jump around through the other stages, too. A subscriber's lifecycle is not always a predictable straight line.

An Integrated View of

Permission

"While the power of permission is what makes email a true powerhouse in the digital world (without permission, email is a mere mortal form of direct marketing), the 'what about this' scenarios that many ask show a big divide."
—Simms Jenkins, Author of *The New Inbox*

Although permission standards in some other countries are much higher and very much a black-or-white proposition, in the U.S. permission has always had plenty of gray areas. That grayness begins with the strength of the permission grant and continues all the way through to the end of the relationship. And in order to maintain a good sender reputation, marketers must define the points at which gray is whitish enough or too blackish for their email program.

Every email relationship begins with a permission grant, which is a combination of an opt-in and opt-in confirmation.

A permission grant's strength =

strength of opt-in

+ strength of opt-in confirmation

+ proximity to purchase.

The **strength of opt-in** is determined by whether the opt-in is active or passive (Rule 2). Active opt-ins include unchecked opt-in boxes and email signup forms where people enter their email address explicitly to receive a brand's promotional emails. Active opt-ins become stronger when subscribers are willing to provide information beyond their email address through a registration process or social sign-in, demonstrating that they have a high interest in the brand.

Passive opt-ins include pre-checked opt-in boxes during a checkout or registration, where the person is automatically subscribed unless they take an action. These opt-ins are weakened when they are hidden in terms and conditions and terms of service agreements, and strengthened when they are highly visible, making the opt-out opportunity hard to miss.

The **strength of opt-in confirmation** is determined by whether it's an active or passive opt-in confirmation. Active opt-in confirmations use the double or confirmed opt-in (COI) process, which considers an opt-in unconfirmed until the subscriber has indicated that they truly intended to opt in by clicking a link in a subscription activation or opt-in confirmation email (Rule 25).

Passive opt-in confirmations look for a subscriber to engage with the emails sent to them early in the relationship as proof that they want to continue receiving emails. For example, for most brands, if a subscriber doesn't open or click any of your welcome emails or other emails during, say, the first 30 days following the opt-in—a time when subscribers are usually the most engaged (Rule 47)—then you should see this as a major red flag and cease mailing them (Rule 4). Consider this confirmed opt-in lite (COIL).

COIL provides protection against spam complaints from subscribers who never intended to opt in or immediately regretted doing so, and limits the effects of reaching inactive accounts intentionally or accidently provided by people. Although COIL doesn't eliminate the risks posed by typo spamtraps and malicious signups, it does lower the risks posed by them by reducing the number of times you email them.

All opt-ins should be confirmed actively via opt-in confirmation emails or passively through near-term engagement.

So while the bar is certainly lower for COIL compared to COI, new subscribers still need to clear that bar in order to stay subscribed. Not clearing this lower bar means the email address represents more of a risk to your deliverability than an opportunity to grow sales.

And lastly, ***proximity to purchase*** is determined by how close the opt-in occurs to a purchase or conversion. Although simply being a customer doesn't constitute an email opt-in, the context in which you secure permission has a significant effect on the value and risk profile of a new subscriber (Rule 28).

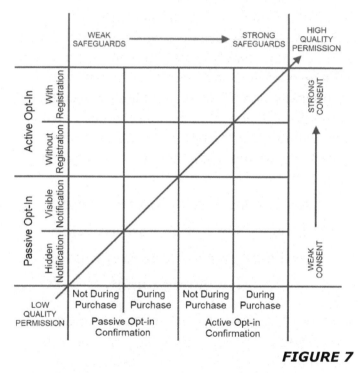

Permission Grant Matrix

FIGURE 7

The strongest scenario would be an opt-in during the checkout process. An opt-in on your homepage email signup form would be slightly weaker; an opt-in on your Facebook page weaker still; and an opt-in on a third-party site the weakest.

Email acquisition sources near your sales and service operations preselect valuable subscribers.

Essentially, the acquisition source says a lot about a subscriber's familiarity with and affinity for your brand. Subscribers who aren't opting in during checkout probably aren't because they're not purchasing often, and subscribers who aren't opting in through your website probably aren't even browsing often. Because of these differences, using the same opt-in and opt-in confirmation methods at different proximities to purchase yields subscribers with different value and risk profiles (Rule 26).

Looking at all three factors, the strongest permission grant would be an active opt-in that occurs during a purchase that is actively confirmed using COI. However, those processes and circumstances would also significantly constrain list growth. Rather, brands generally find that list growth and list quality are balanced when only one of these factors is maximized. (See Fig. 7 on p.248.)

A Goldilocks Permission Grant is not so strong it overly constrains list growth nor so weak it harms deliverability.

Most brands find that the most productive

permission grants involve an active opt-in with passive opt-in confirmation or a passive opt-in with an active opt-in confirmation. The former is used when a person's primary goal is signing up to receive email and the latter is used when the email sign-up is secondary to another goal, such as entering a contest. Both methods result in securing express or explicit consent—the former at the point of opt-in or conversion and the latter through an opt-in confirmation email.

Some brands might also find that a highly visible passive opt-in with a passive opt-in confirmation used during a checkout or registration process is also very effective. Consumers have been well trained to look for these opt-out opportunities, but the risks to quality are slightly higher and deserve extra monitoring because you're only securing implied consent.

Tracking the performance of subscribers that join your list through all the acquisition sources you use allows you to adjust opt-in and opt-in confirmation requirements to ensure that new subscribers are of sufficient quality to keep deliverability risks in check (Rule 26). Doing so also helps you decide whether certain acquisition sources should be further optimized or abandoned.

Of course, the permission grant is just the beginning of a subscriber's time on your email list. Over the course of an email relationship, each subscriber's permission exists in one of six states. (See Fig. 8 on p.252.)

The 6 subscriber statuses are: unconfirmed, subscribed, actively unsubscribed, undeliverable, inactive, and passively unsubscribed.

The introduction of engagement metrics into ISPs' filtering algorithms and the risks posed by spamtraps require that all opt-ins should now be considered *unconfirmed* at their inception. After a subscriber takes the appropriate action to confirm their opt-in, they are considered *subscribed*. Subscribers stay in this state until they unsubscribe actively or passively, or their email address becomes undeliverable.

Subscribers become *actively unsubscribed* through a variety of mechanisms. A subscriber can opt out via your unsubscribe page or preference center—or, if you empower them to, via email reply, letter, call center rep, or native unsubscribe links provided by an email client. They can also opt out with a spam complaint, but you hope the other routes you offer are more appealing.

Subscribers become *passively unsubscribed* when they have been *inactive* for a long time and attempts to reengage them have failed. At this point, they haven't opened or clicked your emails in so long that it's extremely unlikely they'll ever engage again. Accept that permission has expired rather than to risk damage to your sender

Subscriber Status

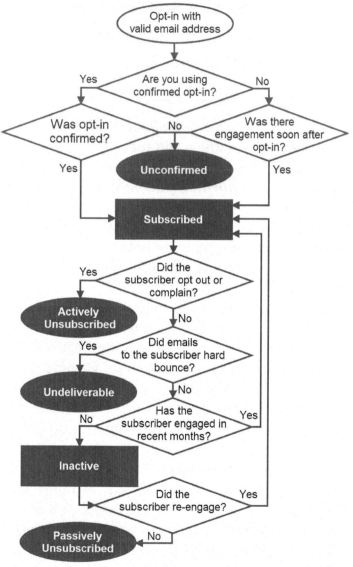

FIGURE 8

reputation by pursuing the increasingly remote possibility that they'll tune in to your emails again (Rule 6).

Although marketers need to define their own deliverability risks around sending email to inactives (Rule 97), when an email address becomes **undeliverable** and hard bounces because the ISP doesn't recognize the account, then you must stop emailing the address immediately. Becoming undeliverable is a form of passively unsubscribing, but it carries much more serious deliverability risks because ISPs have a low tolerance for hard bounces and penalize you if have too many, just like they do when you have too many complaints.

Permission is the foundation of email marketing. Finding the optimal permission grants allows you to grow your list best, and understanding the different states of permission allows you to manage your risks during the lifespan of a subscriber.

An Integrated View of

List Growth

"Having a large list sounds ideal, but it guarantees nothing—except, perhaps, potential deliverability challenges. It certainly doesn't ensure the high ROI for which email is famous."

—Loren McDonald, VP of Industry Relations at Silverpop, An IBM Company

The way list growth is often talked about, you might think that it is synonymous with acquisition—that is, adding more email addresses to your list. However, that's only one of three factors that create meaningful list growth.

List growth is composed of new subscribers added, subscribers lost, and the productivity of your subscribers.

Clearly, adding new subscribers is key to list growth. Ways to achieve this include:

- Making your existing signup forms and opt-in calls-to-action more prominent (Rule 30)

- Simplifying your signup process to boost completion rates (Rule 35)

- Training store, call center, and event staff to better promote the channel and facilitate opt-ins (Rule 25)

- Auditing your acquisition sources to ensure that glitches and malfunctions aren't leading to subscriber loss (Rule 40)

- Using your other marketing channels—paid, owned, leased, granted, and earned media—to promote your email program

- Adding new acquisition sources, particularly those close to your sales and service operations (Rule 28)

Although subscriber acquisition is essential, you can't calculate your **absolute list growth** without considering subscribers lost, too. List churn, which is the number of subscribers lost over a period, directly reduces list growth because a portion of your new subscribers just replaces lost subscribers. If your acquisition rate is higher than your list churn, then your list size increases. However, if your list churn is higher than your acquisition rate, then your list size shrinks.

This might seem obvious, but acknowledging this reality means you can boost your absolute list growth by lowering your list churn or subscriber replacement rate (Rule 110).

A number of activities can reduce your list churn:

- Improve your permission practices (Rules 2, 3, 6–10, & 25) and expectation setting (Rules 31, 34, & 38) so fewer subscribers are lost through spam complaints and unsubscribes early in the email relationship

- Identify the sources of subscribers that churn the least and focus on increasing acquisitions through those sources (Rules 26–28)

- Make your messaging more compelling and relevant by sending more segmented emails (Rule 84), triggered emails (Rule 90), and emails with personalized content (Rule 85)

- Give subscribers other options besides unsubscribing, such as reducing the frequency at which they receive emails (Rule 112)

With most B2C brands sending 150 to 200 broadcast emails a year, even with a good unsubscribe rate of 0.25%, you're seeing more than a third and as much as half of your list churn—and that's not including subscribers that go inactive or become undeliverable.

Because opt-out rates compound with every campaign you send, reducing them even a little has a big effect annually.

But even absolute list growth doesn't give you the full picture. The best measure is to look at *real list growth*, which factors in subscriber productivity. This is essential because replacing high-value subscribers with low-value ones degrades the power of your list, whereas the inverse builds it.

One way to measure real list growth is to factor in subscriber lifetime value (SLV) when looking at your subscriber gains and losses (Rule 12). For instance, if in a month you lost 1,000 subscribers that had an average SLV of $100 and you gained 1,000 subscribers through an acquisition channel that tends to attract subscribers with a SLV of $10, then your real list growth fell significantly even though your absolute list growth was zero.

Expressed in dollars, real list growth measures changes in the overall value of your email list.

Modelling overall list value involves a mix of actual SLVs based on subscribers who have opted out and estimated SLVs based on the acquisition sources of new subscribers and the average historical SLVs of subscribers from those acquisition sources.

Alternatively, for simpler math, you could track *engaged list growth*, which is a measure of the number of subscribers who have engaged with at least one of your emails over a period (Rule 27). For instance, you could look at the number of subscribers each month that have clicked in at least one email. Although this method isn't as good as measuring real list growth, it is a good proxy because most subscribers who are engaged eventually convert.

Conveniently, many of the actions that reduce list churn will also increase engagement and SLV, particularly sending more personalized and targeted messaging. Other activities that grow engagement and SLV include:

- Paying attention to how your email campaigns affect your most valuable subscribers (Rule 14)
- Identifying the behaviors that differentiate high-value subscribers from less valuable ones and encouraging those behaviors

So to get the full picture on the health of your list growth, you need to look at how many subscribers you're adding and how many subscribers you're losing—while factoring in the actual and potential productivity of both groups. Doing so puts the appropriate focus on list quality and ensures you're building an email list that's growing in power, not just in size.

An Integrated View of

Inbox Placement

*"Reaching the inbox is not your goal—
engaging people is."*

—Matt Blumberg, Chairman & CEO of Return Path

Email marketers rightfully obsess over inbox placement, which is their ability to have their emails arrive in subscribers' inboxes rather than being blocked or routed to junk folders. After all, if your subscribers don't receive your emails, then your efforts are all for naught.

However, there's sometimes confusion over what exactly determines a brand's deliverability and who's responsible for it.

Your deliverability is based on your infrastructure, sender reputation, email content and frequency, and send volumes.

Having properly configured *infrastructure* demonstrates to ISPs that you're not a spammer or part of a bot network, which are rarely configured properly. This means publishing WHOIS contact information, setting up a reverse DNS for your IP address, and authenticating your domains.

You should also think of infrastructure more broadly to include the throttling of your email volume to stay within thresholds established by ISPs, as well as bounce management. The latter involves the immediate removal of email addresses that hard bounce because the ISP doesn't recognize the address—often referred to as reaching unknown users—and the removal of email addresses that soft bounce many times because the user's inbox is full, a sign that the account is likely abandoned.

Infrastructure is where your email service provider plays the largest role in the deliverability of your emails.

Although infrastructure is an important component of deliverability (Rule 18), the components that you control—your sender reputation and email content and frequency—have a much greater influence on whether your emails reach your subscribers' inboxes (Rule 19).

Your *sender reputation* is based on your permission practices and the reactions from the recipients of your emails. The foundation is your permission practices and processes, which should aim to add subscribers to your email list that want to hear from you and avoid adding spamtrap addresses and the email addresses of people who don't want to hear from you.

ISPs and spam watchdogs see having a spamtrap—even just one spamtrap—on your email list as a strong sign that you're buying email lists (Rule 10), mailing subscribers that have been inactive for years (Rule 6), and being reckless with your acquisition processes (Rules 2–4, 7–9, 24, & 25). There are flavors of spamtraps associated with each of those activities, all of which can lead to serious deliverability problems.

Negative reactions by recipients also affect your sender reputation. Spam complaints are the most dreaded because they can start to cause problems after your complaint rate exceeds 0.1% (Rule 21). However, ISPs also pay attention to softer indications that mail is unwanted by a user, such as unread emails being deleted.

In part because marketers used to bloat their email lists with inactive subscribers to drive down their complaint rates, ISPs now put considerable emphasis on the positive reactions or engagement of subscribers. Marketers generally measure engagement by opens and clicks, but inbox providers also look at whether their users scroll through, star, forward, reply, or take other actions that demonstrate interest in the emails they receive. This makes it dangerous for brands to hold onto chronically inactive subscribers (Rule 6).

Low engagement rates are nearly as dangerous to your deliverability as high spam complaints.

The emphasis on both complaints and engagement rates by ISPs makes it impossible for marketers to game the system, which now favors a quality over quantity approach to list growth.

Email content and frequency still play a role in deliverability, but it's not as large as in the past. Many years ago, the words you used in your subject line and in your body copy were highly scrutinized by content filters that looked for "spammy" words, such as *free* and *offer*. Although word choice is still given a little weight, now content filtering is much less about the words you use and more about where your emails link to.

Linking to sites with poor reputations or using URL shorteners, which are favored by spammers to obscure the destinations of links, can have a dramatic effect on deliverability. However, if your sender reputation is good and you're linking to only reputable sites, there's no need to censor your word choices in your emails or worry about image-to-text ratios, which was once a major consideration (Rule 22).

An erratic email frequency can also get you in trouble because spammers often operate in random bursts. Seasonal variations that increase volume are okay if they aren't extreme, but long quiet periods followed by short periods of high activity will raise red flags with ISPs. Generally, ISPs like to see consistency in a sender's email volume. Note that how subscribers react to the frequency at which you email them is an entirely separate issue from the sending patterns that ISPs like to see.

One way that smaller brands and brands with uneven mailing patterns can get around frequency issues and the hassles of sender reputation management is by using a shared IP address to send email. This is when several companies send email from the same IP address, which means that they are sharing a single sender reputation.

ESPs that specialize in serving smaller senders typically offer shared IP addresses that they manage, smoothing out sending patterns and monitoring the sender reputation of each of their IP addresses to ensure high deliverability. They also generally require their users to use confirmed opt-ins in order to protect the sender reputation of these shared IP addresses. These ESPs also handle warming up IP addresses, where email volumes going through a new IP address are slowly increased, which gives ISPs an opportunity to get used to this new source of email volume and ascribe it a sender reputation.

Larger senders manage enough volume to have their own dedicated IP addresses, where they control all aspects of their sender reputation.

While that's an advantage of being a large sender, a drawback is that brands with **high volume sends** are scrutinized more by ISPs. Senders with more than 1 million subscribers are more likely to have their emails blocked or junked, just because of the volume of email they send. This is yet another factor to take into consideration when determining how to manage inactive subscribers.

The key takeaway here is that although ESPs play a role in deliverability, most of the responsibility for and power over deliverability resides with senders. Embrace this responsibility to ensure that you're minimizing your risks.

One final dimension of inbox placement is not worrying about where in the inbox your emails arrive, which has become a new concern with the advent of tabbed inboxes (Rule 23). Don't bother asking subscribers to retab your emails or move your messages from one tab to another.

Instead, focus on sending highly relevant messages that your subscribers eagerly anticipate receiving, and then trust that they will organize your emails as best suits them. Left alone, this is what subscribers will do, usually to the benefit of senders.

An Integrated View of

Relevance

"Being useful and interesting and relevant needs to be the least of what your brand is known for, now and in the future."
—Jay Baer, Author of *Youtility*

Expectations are steadily rising in the inbox. Having permission only gets you so far nowadays. Irrelevant and unwanted email is the new spam in the eyes of both consumers and ISPs. Everyone agrees that *relevance* is the solution, but it's often discussed in vague, mystical terms.

Although relevance is indeed in the eye of the beholder, that doesn't mean it's indescribable.

Relevance is created by sending emails that are desired, user-friendly, and valuable.

Emails are ***desired*** when they arrive as expected or requested, when subscribers are in the market to buy your products or services, and at a frequency subscribers don't think excessive. To be desired at the onset of the email relationship, clear and above-board permission practices are the essential first step (Rules 2, 3, & 7–10). Setting expectations during the sign-up process and in your welcome emails (Rules 34 & 41-44) is an important second step.

Later in the email relationship, varying your email frequency according to key selling periods, such as the holiday season, is wise (Rule 80), as is creating an array of triggered emails (Rule 90). Using frequency caps (Rule 94) and allowing subscribers to opt down rather than just opt out (Rule 112) also help ensure emails are desired.

Emails are **user-friendly** when they are easy to scan, read, and navigate across all major platforms (Rules 54 & 55)—a goal that is complicated by the growing number of email-reading devices, particularly mobile ones.

Email text that is difficult to read on smartphones and calls-to-action that can't be accurately tapped with a finger only serve to frustrate subscribers, who are no longer triaging their inbox via mobile and re-opening emails later on their laptops. Emails that are coded poorly so images and grids are broken are also irritating and brand damaging.

Good landing pages are the critical last mile of being user-friendly.

Landing pages should flow seamlessly from the email experience to avoid dampening conversion rates (Rules 100–105).

Emails are **valuable** when they provide the subscriber with content that they find worthwhile, engaging, and compelling as individuals. Let's unpack that statement a little at a time.

First, *worthwhile*. Discounts, deals, and buying-related information are the No. 1 reason people signup for email. If you're a retailer, restaurant, or consumer brand, keep focused on fulfilling those needs. If you're a nonprofit, service, or B2B brand, stay focused on service information and brand-building.

Second, *engaging*. It's also important to engage subscribers who don't consider themselves in the market to make a purchase. Educational and instructional information can provide value to non-purchasers, as well as providing context that makes your products more compelling (Rule 61). Including non-promotional calls-to-action is also important to maintaining engagement between purchases (Rule 63).

Outside voices and cross-channel content can play a powerful role here (Rule 62). A disembodied corporate voice is far less compelling than the voices of customers, staffers, brand advocates, and outside experts—whether in the form of product reviews, testimonials, articles, videos, tweets, or pins.

And third, *compelling as individuals*. Beyond simply delivering what you promised subscribers when they signed up, you can discover what individual subscribers value by collecting demographic information, preferences, purchase history, behavioral data, and social data (Rule 83). And then you use that information to power segmented messages (Rule 84), dynamic content (Rule 85), and triggered emails (Rule 90).

Of course, because brands and their subscriber bases vary so widely, it's not always clear how best to increase relevancy. That's why regularly A/B testing your emails and landing pages is vital (Rules 116–120), because over time you can determine what individual subscribers, key groups of subscribers, and your overall subscriber base responds to best.

An Integrated View of

Email Interaction

*"It's a moment where marketing happens,
where information happens, and where consumers
make choices that affect the success or failure
of nearly every brand in the world."*

—Jim Lecinksi, Author of *Winning the
Zero Moment of Truth*

For most brands, emails are a gateway, not the
destination. Although nice, having your emails
opened or clicked isn't the goal (Rule 16). What
you really want is the conversion—whether it's a
purchase, event registration, mobile app download,
or whatever other high-value action you're driving
subscribers to perform.

To get to that point, it's important to
understand that...

**Email interactions happen in three
semi-connected stages:
envelope content, body content,
and landing page.**

A slim majority of the time, subscribers interact
with emails according to the traditional model,
engaging with each stage in turn and staying

entirely online. (See Fig. 9.)

Stage 1. Before an email is opened, subscribers see the **envelope content**, which is the sender name, subject line, and, in some cases, snippet text.

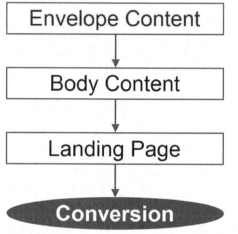

FIGURE 9

The sender name, the text that says who sent the email, has the greatest impact on whether your emails are opened, deleted, or reported as spam, so it should be instantly recognizable by subscribers (Rule 48). Usually, this name is the brand the subscriber signed up to hear from.

The subject line tells subscribers what your email is about. Although creativity has its place, the most effective subject lines are straightforward and predispose openers to engage with the content of an email (Rule 49).

The snippet text appears right after or below the subject line in a number of email clients and is comprised of the first HTML text in the email. Most often pulled from the preheader text, snippet text should extend or reinforce the subject line, giving subscribers more information about the content of the email (Rule 52).

Stage 2. When subscribers open an email, they see the **body content**. Most marketing emails are a mix of text and images, with promotional messages being more image-heavy and transactional messaging more text-heavy. Additionally, lifestyle brands tend to include more images, whereas value brands trend toward more text.

Generally, from top to bottom, emails consist of (see Fig. 3 on p.117):

- Preheader text, which is HTML text that acts like a second subject line (Rule 52)

- A header, which includes your brand's logo (Rule 58)

- A navigation bar, which includes a few links to major entry points to your website (Rule 59)

- A primary message block, which contains the main message of your email

- A secondary message block for an additional call-to-action or two

- A social media bar, with links to your pages on Facebook, Twitter and other social networks (Rule 74)

- A footer, which includes an unsubscribe link and your postal address for CAN-SPAM compliance (Rule 1), disclaimers, and other administrative links and text

Keep in mind that subscribers don't read emails; they scan them (Rule 56). So pay extra attention to headlines; use bullet points and sentence fragments to communicate quickly; and make call-to-action links and buttons clear and obvious (Rule 65). At a glance, subscribers should know what you want them to do next and what's in it for them.

Stage 3. Landing pages are the web pages, apps, and other destinations subscribers arrive at after clicking the calls-to-action in your emails. A strong connection between the email content and the landing page reassures subscribers that they've arrived at the right place (Rule 101). For instance, consider repeating headlines and images from the email on the landing page.

From there, your checkout, registration, and other processes will hopefully carry the subscriber through to conversion—which is the ultimate goal of most email interactions (Rules 16, 102, & 103).

This traditional model, however, is being upended.

Multichannel environments and inbox capabilities allow subscribers to act in ways that are very difficult to track.

Track progression and influence at each stage is becoming more difficult because of the growing number of scenarios that can play out when subscribers bypass one or more stages (Rule 15). (See Fig. 10.)

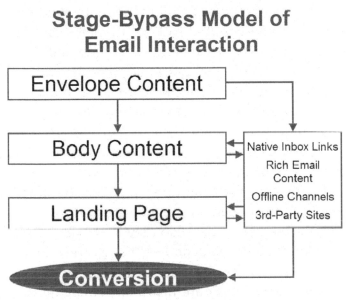

Stage-Bypass Model of Email Interaction

FIGURE 10

For instance, a subscriber could read the envelope content about a sale you're holding and, rather than clicking through, open a new browser window and type in your website's URL. Or they could hop in their car and drive to your store, if you're promoting a store sale. Or they might call your call center and make a purchase that way. All are positive, desirable actions, but they're also difficult to measure because the subscriber neither opened nor clicked the email.

Similarly, a subscriber might search for a hashtag in your subject line on social media and join the conversation there. Again, a positive action was driven with an open or click.

Body content can lead subscribers to skip the landing page associated with your email's calls-to-action. They can forego clicking through and instead search for your brand or product in a search engine, visit your brand on social media, or open your mobile app to take action.

Moreover, rich email content, such as HTML5 video, is pulling content into emails that previously would have been on a landing page. Such capabilities are good for inbox providers because they keep their users in the inbox, and they're good for marketers because they lower the barriers to taking the desired action—although they do effectively limit the response to a single action.

Native inbox links are also short-circuiting the traditional flow of email interactions. Enabled by marketers, these links appear as part of the email client interface and perform a variety of actions. These include subject line quick links that let subscribers click through to the landing page for the primary call-to-action of the email without opening the email.

These also include native unsubscribe links, which allow subscribers opt out without visiting the sender's unsubscribe page or preference center.

Generally more trusted than the unsubscribe links offered by senders, these links promise the efficiency of a Report Spam button, but without harming the sender reputation of the sender.

All of this is to say that email interactions are getting trickier to follow and therefore...

Whatever return on investment you think your email program is generating, it's likely significantly higher.

Withhold studies and other tests can help you develop a fairly accurate ROI model, but ultimately returns are a spectrum that goes from easy-to-measure hard ROI to difficult-to-measure soft ROI.

However, no matter how disrupted the flow of an email interaction becomes, the part that will always have the greatest influence on whether an email interaction is successful is what happens before Stage 1.

The Stage Zero of Email Interaction is your subscriber's past experiences with your email program and brand in general.

That's why your sender name is so critical (Rule 48). It's not just about being recognized as a brand they know, as a brand that they have an email relationship with. The sender name represents all the recent interactions they've had with you—both online and offline. Positive recent experiences bode well for obtaining your next open, click, and conversion sooner rather than later.

An Integrated View of

Rendering

"Building great emails that perform across the myriad of clients and devices is difficult and, oftentimes, extraordinarily frustrating. It involves working with markup at which most designers would cringe and hacking your way to success."
—Jason Rodriguez, Author of *Modern HTML Email*

Website developers have it hard. They have to deal with a number of environments equal to the number of operating systems times the number of browsers times the number of device types. However...

Email rendering is exponentially more complex than website rendering.

Email designers and coders have all of those combinations times the number of email clients—of which there are an increasing number. All these component layers means email coding is an extreme exercise in finding the lowest common denominator of coding that works across every environment combination (Rule 54).

This rendering environment is complicated further by the fact that updates in any of these layers can potentially cause significant changes in how your emails render. Not only are there regular updates in operating systems (OS), apps, and browsers, but also minor and often unannounced tweaks are made to webmail interfaces.

Past instances of this have led to images in emails suddenly having a 1-pixel border; inbox display preferences overriding the default styling of background, text, and link colors; and special characters like ™, ©, and ♥ being converted into 16x16-pixel emoji images. In those instances—and many others—email marketers were left to scramble for workarounds to regain control over how their emails looked.

Because your emails could potentially look different in Gmail using Firefox and Gmail using Internet Explorer and because of unannounced changes, it's highly recommended that you use a rendering preview tool—or at the very least set up test accounts to check the rendering of your emails regularly.

Paying attention to every possible OS-app-browser-client-device combination is nearly impossible—and a poor use of your time. Analyze your subscriber base and focus your attention on the most popular combinations, while only occasionally auditing how your emails render on the others.

Trying to have your emails render identically in every email client is similarly pointless. Again, focus on the environments most popular with your audience and then be prepared to accept less than perfect rendering in the least popular environments.

The Age of Mobile has fundamentally and forever changed email design.

Although mobile devices are a huge opportunity for email marketers in general, it has created a huge design challenge because HTML emails have historically been designed for desktop viewing. In less than a decade, the percentage of emails read on mobile devices rose from a small minority to a slim majority, sparked by the launch of the iPhone, which was the first mobile device to render HTML emails.

This shift will lead to desktop-centric email design—characterized by multi-column layouts, small text, and high link densities—being replaced by mobile-aware design and responsive design (Rule 54). Mobile-aware design uses basic techniques to create a single email that functions well across a range of screen sizes but is deferential to smartphones; whereas responsive design uses a variety of advanced techniques to serve up versions or renderings of an email that are optimized for particular screen resolutions or email clients.

Responsive design holds the most promise because the number of screen sizes and the spread between the smallest and largest screen sizes is likely to continue to grow. Going forward, the proliferation of wearables, such as optical head-mounted displays and smart watches, will drive the small end of the screen size spectrum.

Beyond optimizing the email experience for the screen size, responsive design also enables you to create device-targeted content, where the content of your email differs depending on the device it's read on. For instance, mobile readers would see a banner promoting your mobile app, whereas desktop readers of the same email would not. Or phablet users would see promotions for a new phablet or related accessories while readers of the same email on other devices would see something entirely different.

Beyond those combinations and possibilities, emails also have to contend with image blocking. A significant number of inbox providers still block the images of emails by default. For the images in your emails to be displayed, subscribers have to enable or turn on images, which they can do for individual emails or for all emails from a particular sender.

So long as this is the case, you will need to use defensive design tactics—including using *alt* text and HTML text—to ensure the graceful degradation of your emails (Rule 55).

In total, installed app-based email environments like Outlook have four layers, while webmail environments like Gmail.com have five layers. (See Fig. 11 on p.281.) That's a lot of different possible combinations across each of those layers.

Environment Layers Compound Email Rendering Complexity

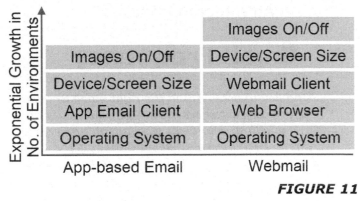

FIGURE 11

This massive level of rendering variability is due to the fact that...

Email is an open platform with no universal coding standards.

The fact that email can be sent from and read on so many platforms is what makes email so ubiquitous and its reach so powerful, but rendering issues and deliverability concerns are the biggest downsides of email as a marketing channel. Luckily, the pros far outweigh the cons.

An Integrated View of

Email Frequency

"The key to establishing the right email frequency with your customers, as in every aspect of email marketing, is to plan, test, adapt, analyze, and refine. Each marketer will find that different rules apply to different customers."

—Simms Jenkins, Author of *The Truth about Email Marketing*

How many emails a month do you send your subscribers? Answering this question used to be pretty straightforward because nearly all your subscribers received the same number of broadcast emails from you.

Now this question often prompts many more questions:

- What month is it?

- Do you mean my new subscribers or subscribers who have already been onboarded?

- Are you referring to my active subscribers or inactive subscribers?

- Do you mean my loyalty program subscribers or ones that are in another program?

- Should I exclude transactional and post-purchase emails from that count?

You ask these questions because marketers now send many more types of emails and send them in a much more targeted fashion. (See Fig. 12 on p.284.)

A subscriber's email frequency is the sum of broadcast, seasonal, segmented, triggered, and transactional emails.

Each subscriber's baseline email frequency is determined by their selections when they sign up. If no options are offered, then everyone starts with the same baseline. However, if you offer different topic selections or different newsletter mailstreams, those picks will decide a subscriber's baseline broadcast email frequency (Rule 34).

Seasonality is the first variable that affects the baseline email frequency throughout the year. You should be sending subscribers more email during your hot selling periods—whether it's the holiday season for retailers, the run up to Valentine's Day and Mother's Day for florists, or the winter months for travel companies (Rule 80).

More than likely, demand for your products and services isn't consistent all year long, so your email volume shouldn't be consistent either. Email volume changes should roughly mirror changes in your revenue. Send extra emails during the times of the year when you're selling the most, and you'll sell even more.

The Email Pyramid

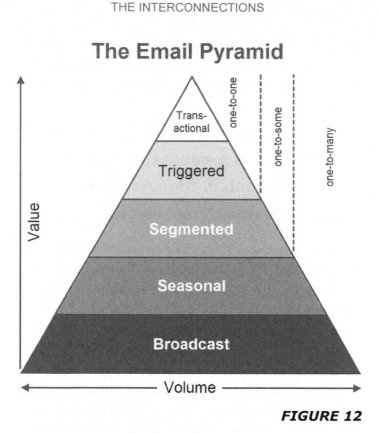

FIGURE 12

You can experiment to find the optimal baseline email frequency for your program by seeing how your subscribers respond in aggregate to increases in email volume. After you find that sweet spot for your broadcast and seasonal volume, it's then all about the individual.

Just like seasonal email volume should mirror swings in purchase patterns...

For individual subscribers,

the frequency at which they receive

emails should mirror their level
of engagement.

Put another way, a subscriber's engagement is a feedback loop that tells you "I really enjoy getting your emails, so feel free to email me more often" or "I'm not enjoying the emails you're sending me so send me something else or email me less often." (See Fig. 13 on p.286.)

For your most engaged subscribers, the safest ways to respond to their positive feedback is to send them segmented and triggered messages, plus dynamic content in your broadcast and seasonal emails. Your moderately engaged subscribers will also benefit from these tactics, but these are key to interacting with your most valuable subscribers because they will be giving you many more opportunities to respond.

Use browsing and purchase patterns, as well as preferences that are directly stated through a preference center or progressive profiling (Rule 83), to send segmented emails (Rule 84). Those same data points can also be used to create targeted dynamic content within broadcast, seasonal, and other messages (Rule 85). These techniques require marketers to recognize subscribers' behaviors and manually respond with messaging on a one-to-some level.

Additionally, set up an array of events that trigger additional messages that arrive when subscribers are most responsive (Rule 90). If all

Subscriber Types by Email Volume

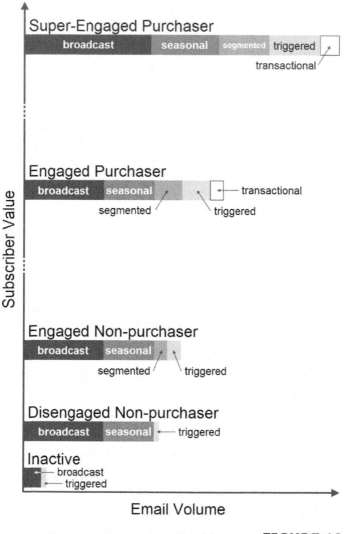

FIGURE 13

that is successful, then you'll also be sending transactional emails, which can themselves generate additional sales (Rule 89). These techniques require marketers to set up automated messages that are delivered on a one-to-one level to subscribers.

Serving subscribers on a one-to-one level is particularly critical because these communications convert at a high level.

Highly sophisticated email marketers generate most of their revenue from triggered and transactional emails.

At the other end of the engagement spectrum are your inactive subscribers, those who haven't opened or clicked in many months (Rule 97). Their lack of engagement—or negative feedback—should dictate that they receive emails less frequently, which helps your deliverability (Rule 98).

However, you should try to reengage these subscribers with triggered win-back emails. If those fail, a subscriber's chronic inactivity should eventually trigger a re-permission email (Rule 99).

Of course, most of your subscribers will fall between these two engagement extremes. There will be active subscribers who occasionally convert and active subscribers who don't appear to convert because they're converting offline or influencing someone else to convert.

Looking at the full spectrum, you'll find that your subscriber base is composed of several different types of subscribers, including inactives, disengaged non-purchasers, engaged non-purchasers, engaged purchasers, and super-engaged purchasers.

Catering to and optimizing your messaging and message volume to each of these types is key to serving them best and maximizing their value as a subscriber and customer.

At the broadest level, how well you're serving these subscriber types is measured by your average subscriber lifetime value (Rule 12). However, an important secondary measure is how effective you are at converting inactives and disengaged non-purchasers into engaged non-purchasers, engaged non-purchasers into engaged purchasers, and engaged purchasers into super-engaged purchasers.

Although converting subscribers up from one type to the next is not easy to accomplish, when marketers do so, the rewards grow exponentially.

The Last Word on the Interconnections

The Team Rule

Depending on the size of your organization and the industry that you're in, the responsibilities for email marketing might fall entirely on you or a small group of coworkers. Don't let yourself get siloed and isolated.

Email marketing works best as part of a comprehensive cross-channel strategy that receives input from multiple sources—including the web, store, merchandising, social, customer service, management, and broader marketing teams.

That fact gives us our third Power Rule, *The Team Rule:*

Email marketing is a team sport,

where you have to collaborate with

and understand other teams,

and vice versa.

The *vice versa* in this rule is particularly critical. Not only do you need to educate yourself about the objectives and concerns of your colleagues, you need to educate them about email marketing best practices so they understand your objectives and concerns.

I hope this book helps you to do that—particularly with executives, who can take your email program to new heights with their support or completely hobble it with unintentionally harmful demands.

PART III

The Future

Email marketing is a living machine that's always changing and evolving. In this final part, let's look at some of the developments that are likely to occur in the coming years.

The Only Constant

10 Ways Email Marketing Will Change in the Decade Ahead

"As a company, you need to get to the future first, ahead of your customers, and be ready to greet them when they arrive."

—Marc Benioff, Founder, Chairman, & CEO of salesforce.com

Because it's well established among consumers and the vendor community, people like to refer to the email channel as *mature*. However, don't mistake that to mean the email channel is static. It's far from it.

Over the past decade:

- The definition of *spam* has been completely redefined because of ISPs successfully blocking malicious, unwanted email

- Social media has given marketers new content for their emails and given subscribers new ways to share email content

- ISPs began factoring engagement rates into their filtering algorithms, forcing marketers to overhaul their list building and list hygiene practices;

- Email automation tools have allowed brands to

respond quickly to subscriber actions with the right triggered message

- The iPhone and all the mobile devices that followed have radically reshaped email design and brought a newfound immediacy to email

- The emergence of Big Data has allowed brands take personalization and targeting to the next level

The next decade of email marketing will surely be just as dynamic. Here are some of the ways that email marketing is likely to evolve in the years ahead:

Email rendering will become even more complex as the market for wearables and the internet of things take off. Some devices will be able to display full emails, whereas others will show only subject lines, making clarity within envelope copy even more important.

Because of shrinking device sizes, the verbal navigation of inboxes and the ***audio transcription*** of emails will become issues at some point. Email design concerns will then include determining which content is read out and picking the appropriate voice "fonts" and intonation "styles."

Responsive design will take on entirely new dimensions because of the rise of wearables and the internet of things.

Image blocking will cease to be an issue. ISPs will no longer see it as a security issue and their ability to block spam will make the practice unnecessary.

The trend toward **_inboxes within inboxes_** will continue, primarily through the further rollout of tabbed inboxes that partition inboxes into sub-inboxes. Simply put, consumers can manage their email more easily when similar messages are grouped together rather than mixed in among the rest. Grouping emails by type allows email users get in a shopping or social frame of mind, for instance, and then deal with all the emails of that sort. This is good for email users, email marketers, and inbox providers.

Relatedly, email inboxes will slowly continue to take on more communication functionality, creeping toward becoming a **_unified inbox_**, where emails, texts, social updates, voicemails, and other messages will comingle just one click away from each other. Mobile devices have provided a template for how to do this, with alerts and notifications all appearing on lockout screens.

Along with mixing of media types, the inbox will gain more **_rich email content_**. People will be able to play videos, browse product assortments, and make purchases—all without leaving their inboxes. Moreover, all content will be up to date at the time it's opened. Following in the wake of social and mobile, this is likely the next big wave of disruption in email marketing.

The emails of the future will be much more like sending subscribers a microsite than a static message.

Personalization, segmentation, and triggered emails will be used at much higher levels than they are today thanks to marketers' ability to tap **Big Data**, harness cross-channel integration, and leverage sophisticated digital marketing platforms. As a result, email marketing will become even more profitable—even after taking into account rising production and platform costs.

Relatedly, data collection will likely be much more transparent and permission-based. Email preference centers will morph into **communication preference and profile centers**, where consumers can modify their cross-channel messaging preferences and edit personal information collected about themselves.

This will largely come about because of changes in **consumer attitudes toward privacy**. More companies will incorporate privacy protections into products. In fact, device and software companies will eventually compete on their default privacy features.

Along the way, it seems inevitable that new **privacy and data security legislation and regulations**, driven by consumer outrage over continued data breaches and identity theft, will be passed. Like CAN-SPAM, any new laws will likely be aimed at the most egregious violators. However, the laws will make brands think much more strategically about the consumer information they collect and store and the appropriate level of security to protect that data. The courts are also likely to get involved, recognizing that consumers have rights regarding information collected about them.

Given the constant change in our industry, especially on the technology front, it pays to be proactive. If you wait until there are five case studies in hand before implementing or even testing a particular change, you will have likely sacrificed a year or more of competitive advantage.

As an email marketer,

if you're not living at least

six months in the future,

you're in trouble.

Content schedules, testing schedules, and—most importantly—technology upgrade and rollout schedules are all critical to competing effectively in the email marketing industry. The future of email is always in motion, so you always have to be chasing it. Thankfully, the velocity of email marketing is so fast you have nearly unparalleled opportunities to fail small and then quickly recover and improve.

Despite all the changes that I foresee, the one thing I don't see happening is email being disrupted and overtaken by another communication channel. Some people said social and mobile were the new kings of communication, but in the end those channels only made email more relevant and more entrenched. (Some even said RSS was the heir-apparent.)

Email hasn't been dethroned because no other channel can match its scale, richness of message, one-to-one capabilities, or open platform. That last point is critical and why Facebook, a closed platform, will never become large enough to threaten email.

The only thing that could threaten email would be another open platform—possibly an open platform social network with email at its core. Email's core technologies are more than a decade old, so this new platform might come from a major refresh of the underlying technology.

Similar to the way open standards forced AOL (the market leading inbox provider in the 1990s) to eventually allow its users to email non-AOL users, the same thing might happen with social media. When, or if, this happens, you can expect a new edition of *Email Marketing Rules* to follow shortly thereafter.

The Last Word on the Future

The Evolving Rule

Books are a great way to appreciate the big picture, understand the general state of the industry, and get a firm grasp on the fundamentals. However, because email marketing is a dynamic and rapidly evolving channel, books are not the ideal way to stay up to date.

That fact brings us to our fourth and final Power Rule, *The Evolving Rule:*

Be constantly learning and experimenting because email marketing is always evolving.

This is only the beginning of your email marketing journey—a journey that frankly never ends. I've been doing email marketing research for a decade and I can honestly say that there's no shortage of new trends, tactics, and tools to explore.

I hope that *Email Marketing Rules* has helped

propel you on your journey by sparking your imagination and getting you excited about improving your program.

Before you do that, however, here are three final steps you should take:

1st

If you enjoyed this book and think others would benefit from reading it, please submit a short review on <u>Amazon.com</u>. Reviews have a huge impact on the visibility of a book, and are especially meaningful for independent authors like myself.

2nd

Visit <u>EmailMarketingRules.com</u> and sign up to receive updates via email to get my latest thoughts on everything email marketing—including new email marketing research, current examples of inspiring email campaigns, and timely discussions about the issues affecting our industry.

You'll also find links to follow me on social media.

3rd

Connect with others in the email marketing community, starting with some of the wonderful experts who regularly inspire me, who I list along with their Twitter handles in the Acknowledgments on the next page.

Follow them. And follow the people that they interact with.

If you're not on Twitter, track them down on LinkedIn and connect with them there.

The email marketing community is very active, surprisingly open, and extremely welcoming, so I wholeheartedly encourage you to jump in and join the conversation.

And although social networks are wonderful, attending conferences can be even more rewarding. Conferences offer educational content and great networking opportunities, allowing you to meet face-to-face and shake hands with the folks you've connected with online.

I wish you all the best with your email marketing efforts and hope to see you online or at an event soon.

Acknowledgments

Brilliant People to Whom I'm Grateful

This book is the culmination of a thousand conversations. Some of those were live, via email, on Twitter, or through comments on my blogs. Others were silent conversations I had by reading the articles, whitepapers, and blog posts of my peers.

I am grateful for all the conversations I've had over the years, but I am especially grateful for those I've had with...

Loren McDonald (@LorenMcDonald)
Simms Jenkins (@SimmsJenkins)
Kristina Huffman (@krudz)
Justine Jordan (@meladorri)
Wacarra Yeomans (@wac_intosh)
Morgan Stewart (@trendlinei)
Joel Book (@joelbook)
George Bilbrey (@returnpath)
John Caldwell (@jacaldwell)
Anne Holland (@anneholland55)
Dela Quist (@DelaQuist)
Anna Yeaman (@stylecampaign)
Derek Harding (@innovyx)

Ben Chestnut (@benchestnut)
Jeanne Jennings (@jeajen)
Scott Hardigree (@indiescott)
Ryan Phelan (@ryanpphelan)
Andrew Kordek (@andrewkordek)
Kara Trivunovic (@ktrivunovic)
Dave Chaffey (@davechaffey)
Tim Watson (@tawatson)
Jordan Cohen (@jcohen808)
Andrew Bonar (@andrewbonar)
Jordie van Rijn (@jvanrijn)
Ros Hodgekiss (@yarrcat)
Elliot Ross (@iamelliot)
Matthew Vernhout (@emailkarma)
Al Iverson (@aliverson)
Spencer Kollas (@spencerkollas)
Stephanie Miller (@StephanieSAM)
Dennis Dayman (@ddayman)
Laura Atkins (@wise_laura)
Alex Williams (@alexcwilliams)

...as well as DJ Waldow, Justin Premick, Heather Goff, Lisa Harmon, Dylan Boyd, Jeanniey Mullen, and the late, great Stefan Pollard. Thank you all for shaping, confirming, and challenging my views.

For helping me complete this book, I'm exceedingly grateful to my amazing editors, Mark Brownlow (@markbrownlow) and Aaron Smith, whose insights, guidance, and suggestions were absolutely invaluable. Thanks also to Andrea Smith (@andreasmith77) for designing the book cover and creating the illustrations, and to Brian Walls for his keen copyediting.

Special thanks to Jay Baer (@jaybaer) for all of his inspiring work and for writing a wonderful foreword to this book.

I'm very thankful to have the support of my colleagues at the Salesforce ExactTarget Marketing Cloud, in particular Kyle Lacy (@kyleplacy) and Jeff Rohrs (@jkrohrs).

I'd also like to acknowledge Michael Pollan, whose book *Food Rules* strongly influenced the format and style of my book (and perhaps influenced my choice of title as well).

And finally, my most heartfelt thanks go to my wonderful wife, Kate, who supported and encouraged me during all the weekends and late nights I spent writing this book and who inspired me to write it in the first place. Thanks, Love.

Glossary

Common Email Marketing Terms

50/50 split test: Exposing half your subscribers to one version of an email or landing page and the other half of your subscribers to another version and seeing which version performs better to inform future decisions; *also see **A/B testing** and **10/10/80 split test***

10/10/80 split test: Exposing 10% of your subscribers to one version of an email or landing page and another 10% of your subscribers to another version, seeing which version performs better, and then exposing the remaining 80% of your subscribers to that winning version; *also see **50/50 split test** and **A/B testing***

above the fold: The portion of an email that displays before a subscriber scrolls; *also see **below the fold***

absolute list growth: A measure of the change in the number of subscribers on an email list over a period of time; also see engaged list growth and real list growth

A/B testing: Exposing a portion of your subscribers to one version of an email or landing page and another portion of your subscribers to another version and seeing which version performs better; *also see **50/50 split test** and **10/10/80 split test***

acquisition: *see **list building***

active consent: Permission indicated when a person explicitly acts to indicate that they want you to add them to your email list (e.g., checking an unchecked box); *also see **passive consent***

active unsubscribe: When subscribers opt out either through an unsubscribe mechanism provided by the sender or through one provided by their ISP, including Report Spam buttons

alt **text:** Text coded into an *<img>* tag that is displayed when the image is blocked and when recipients mouse over the image, although support isn't consistent

animated gif: An image file that displays multiple images sequentially over time, sometimes in a loop

apology email: A message sent in response to an error or mishap

app-based email: An email client that's installed on a device; *also see* **webmail**

back-in-stock email notification: Sent after the product is back in stock, this triggered email is sent to those who opt in on an out-of-stock product page to receive notification when that particular item is available again

below the fold: The portion of an email that displays only after a subscriber scrolls; *also see* **above the fold**

best practices: Those practices that generally produce the best results or minimize risk

blacklist: A list of senders of spam typically maintained by an independent organization that is used by ISPs to determine whether and where to deliver email

blocked: When an ISP prevents your emails from being delivered to their users

body content: The text, images, and other content inside your email that becomes visible when opened

body copy: *see* **body content**

bounced: When email is rejected by an internet service provider because it was sent to an unknown email address (hard bounce) or because of a temporary condition like the recipient's mailbox being full (soft bounce)

broadcast email: An email that is sent to all subscribers

browse abandonment email: A message sent to an

individual subscriber in response to that person browsing certain pages of your website but not making a purchase

browse retargeting email: *see* ***browse abandonment email***

bulked: *see* ***junked***

call-to-action (CTA): What a message asks a subscriber to do, but more specifically the buttons and links subscribers click to take action

challenger: During an A/B test, the design or process that you think will be an improvement to your existing design or process; *also see* ***champion***

champion: During an A/B test, your existing design or process; *also see* ***challenger***

cinemagraph: A picture composed of both static images and one or more animated gifs, which give motion, often subtle, to a small portion of the overall picture

click: When a subscriber selects a link or linked image in an email with a mouse, trackpad, tap of a touchscreen, etc. and visits the associated landing page

click reach: The percentage of your subscribers who clicked at least one of your emails over a period of time (e.g., over the past month or quarter)

click-to-open rate: Percentage of subscribers who opened an email that also clicked the content inside, which is calculated by dividing clicks by opens

confirmed opt-in (COI): The process of sending a subscription activation or opt-in confirmation email to a new subscriber that requires them to click a link in that email to confirm their signup or else receive no additional emails

content filtering: When an ISP evaluates an email's subject line and other content as part of its process to decide whether and where the mail should be delivered

Controlling the Assault of Non-Solicited Pornography and Marketing Act of 2003 (CAN-SPAM): A law regulating commercial email messaging that forbids deceptive messaging, requires senders to include a working unsubscribe link and their mailing address in every email they send, and requires senders to honor opt-out requests quickly, among other things

conversion: When a subscriber clicks through an email and then makes a purchase, registers for an event, or takes another action requested by the email

conversion reach: The percentage of your subscribers that have converted through at least one of your emails over a period of time (e.g., over the past month or quarter)

dedicated IP address: An IP address from which only one company sends email, making that company solely responsible for the sender reputation of that address; *also see* ***shared IP address***

defensive design: Design techniques that allow an email to communicate its message effectively when images are blocked

deliverability: All of the issues involved with getting commercial emails delivered to their intended recipients' inboxes

delivered: When email makes it to the intended recipient's inbox or junk folder, as opposed to being blocked

desktop-centric design: Design techniques that create emails optimized for viewing on large monitors, typically with small, tightly clustered links and buttons

device-targeted content: Using responsive email design to target subscribers with different content depending on the device that the email is displayed on

double entry confirmation: Requiring a would-be subscriber to enter their email address again in a *confirm email address* field on a subscription form and requiring that the two entries match in order to reduce entry errors

double opt-in: *see* ***confirmed opt-in***

dynamic content: A portion of an email that contains different content for different groups of subscribers or individuals based on their geography, demographics, behavior, or other factors

earned media: Media content produced by media outlets, bloggers, consumers, and other end users of a brand's products or services about that brand that's distributed via any platform, such as publicity, social sharing, word of mouth, and ratings and reviews; *also see **granted media**, **leased media**, **owned media**, and **paid media***

email acquisition source: The form or mechanism through which a subscriber opts in, or the ad, sign, or other vehicle that causes them to opt in

email authentication: A variety of methods that help ISPs accurately identify email sent by a brand, including Domain Keys Identified Mail (DKIM), Sender Policy Framework (SPF), and Domain-based Message Authentication, Reporting & Conformance (DMARC)

email automation: Triggered emails, personalization, dynamic content, and other tools that send emails or add content to emails on a one-to-one or one-to-some basis without manual intervention according to rules established by a brand

email client: An application or web interface that displays emails and allows users to reply, forward, and interact with the content of the message

email list: A list of the email addresses and other records associated with your subscribers

email metrics: Measurements of the effectiveness of your email marketing program

email reader: see *email client*

email service provider (ESP): A commercial provider of email marketing services that allows their clients to manage their email lists, send messages, track the response of message recipients, and process opt-ins and opt-outs, among other capabilities

email template: Preformatted email file that includes all the elements you want to appear in every email and spots for content that changes from email to email

engaged list growth: A measure of the change in the number of subscribers who have engaged with at least one of your emails over a period of time; *also see absolute list growth and real list growth*

engagement: Opens, clicks, and other positive indications that a subscriber is finding value in receiving emails from a brand

envelope content: The portion of an email that's visible to subscribers before they open it (i.e., sender name, subject line, etc.)

express consent: *see active consent*

expressed preferences: The topics, activities and other things that subscribers tell you they are interested in; *also see implied preferences*

feedback loop (FBL): A mechanism through which ISPs and other inbox providers notify email senders of spam complaints by their subscribers, allowing senders to unsubscribe those subscribers

first-name personalization: Dynamically adding an email recipient's first name to either the envelope or body copy of an email

footer: The HTML text at the bottom of an email that includes the promotional fine print, legal language, unsubscribe link, mailing address, and other details

forward to a friend (FTAF): Providing a link in your email that takes subscribers to a form that allows them to forward all or a portion of your email or a particular message promoted in your email to one or more people that they know

freemail: An email account that is available for free from Yahoo, AOL, Gmail, Outlook.com, or another ISP

geofence: A boundary set up around a physical location that's used to trigger messaging when a subscriber crosses it, either coming or going

geolocation-based messaging: Using a person's mobile device or some other method to identify their physical location and then sending them email, push notifications, and other messaging because they approached or departed a predefined physical area

gift services footer: A secondary content block that is typically positioned just before the footer that pulls together links to gift guides, order-by deadlines, return policies and other important seasonal buying information

global filtering: When an ISP junks and blocks all email sent by a brand to any of its email users; *also see subscriber-level filtering*

granted media: Media content produced by a brand that's distributed to an audience the brand developed via an open platform controlled by multiple third parties, such as email and SMS; *also see earned media, leased media, owned media* and *paid media*

graphical text: Text that is part of an image; *also see HTML text*

header: The upper portion of an email that includes your brand's logo

hero: *see primary message*

holiday header: A temporary, holiday-themed header design that supports the seasonal messaging of your emails

HTML text: Text from a limited number of fonts that are universally or widely supported across email clients; *also see graphical text*

image blocking: When ISPs or subscribers don't allow the images in an email to load

implied consent: *see passive consent*

implied preferences: The topics, activities, and other things that subscribers indicate they are interested in based on their interactions with your brand; *also see expressed preferences*

inactive subscriber: A subscriber who has not opened or clicked in any of your emails in a long time; the opposite of an active or engaged subscriber

inactivity: When a subscriber has not opened or clicked in any of your emails in a long time

inbox placement rate: The percentage of emails sent by a brand or from an IP address that reaches their intended recipients' inboxes, as opposed to being blocked or junked

internet service provider (ISP): Shorthand term for providers of web-based, desktop, and mobile email inboxes that send, store, and organize messages for users and manage and block spam (e.g., Gmail, Outlook, etc.)

IP address warming: A process of building up a sender reputation on a new IP address by gradually ramping up the volume of email sent from it

junked: When emails are routed to a recipient's junk or spam folder by an ISP

landing page: Webpage, app, and any other destination that subscribers are directed to when they click a call-to-action in one of your emails

leased media: Media content produced by a brand that's distributed to an audience the brand developed via a closed platform controlled by a third party, such as Facebook, Twitter, and mobile app platforms; *also see earned media, granted media, owned media,* and *paid media*

list building: The process of adding email addresses to your mailing list

list churn: Subscribers lost to unsubscribes, spam complaints, and bounces from email addresses that no longer work

list hygiene: Ensuring that your email list is free of invalid and undeliverable email addresses, role-based email addresses, spam traps, unconfirmed email addresses, and chronically inactive subscribers

list rental: Having a message sent on your behalf to an email list owned by someone else

live content: Images and other email content that vary

based on when the email is opened, what kind of device it's opened on, and other factors

loaded weight: The file size of the HTML coding of an email plus the total file size of all images used in the email

mailing list: *see email list*

mailstream: The emails resulting from a single opt-in or preference selection

malicious opt-outs: When a person uses your opt-out page to unsubscribe someone else without that person's consent

malicious signups: When a person signs up to receive email from a brand using an address they know to be false, inaccurate, or spam traps for the explicit purpose of harming that brand's sender reputation

mobile-aware email design: Basic design techniques that create a single email that functions well across a range of screen sizes, but is deferential to smartphones

multivariate testing: Similar to A/B testing, except multiple variations in an email or landing page are tested simultaneously, which requires lots of data to do accurately

native inbox links: Enabled by marketers, these links appear as part of the email client interface and perform a variety of actions

navigation bar: A row of links to important pages on your website

newsjacking: Leveraging the popularity of a news story, event, or cultural phenomena to promote yourself or your company

onboarding: The process of familiarizing new subscribers with your email program and your brand using your signup confirmation page and welcome emails

open: When the images in an email are loaded or rendered, which typically happens when a subscriber views an email with images enabled

open reach: The percentage of your subscribers that

have opened at least one of your emails over a period of time (e.g., over the past month or quarter)

opt down: When a subscriber chooses to receive a brand's emails less frequently

opt-in confirmation email: Part of a confirmed or double opt-in, this email requires a new subscriber to click a link in the email to confirm their signup or else they receive no additional emails

opt-in confirmation page: Webpage or app messaging that follows a successful email signup

opt-in email marketing: Sending email only to those who have given you permission to do so; *also see opt-out email marketing*

opt out: *see unsubscribe*

opt-out email marketing: Sending email to those who have not given you permission to do so and requiring them to unsubscribe or mark your emails as spam if they don't want to receive future emails; *also see opt-in email marketing*

opt-out page: *see unsubscribe page*

opt-out process: *see unsubscribe process*

opt over: When a subscriber opts into one of your other channels, such as social or mobile, during your email unsubscribe process

opt up: When a subscriber opts into additional mailstreams from a brand, whether via a preference center, loyalty program, or sister brands

owned media: Media content that's produced by a brand that's distributed to an audience the brand developed via a closed platform controlled by the brand, such as a brand's website, brochures, in-store signage, and events; *also see earned media, granted media, leased media,* and *paid media*

paid media: Media content produced by a brand that's distributed to an audience developed by a third party via a closed platform controlled by that third party, such as

TV ads, radio ads, newspaper ads, billboards, search ads, and display ads; *also see **earned media, granted media, leased media,** and **owned media***

passive consent: Permission indicated when a person does not act to keep you from adding them to your email list (e.g., not unchecking a pre-checked box); *also see* **active consent**

passive unsubscribe: When subscribers effectively opt out by either not engaging with your emails for a very long time or by abandoning their email account altogether, causing your emails to eventually hard bounce

permission: Actively or passively agreeing to receive promotional email

personalization: Including information that's unique to the recipient in the subject line or body copy of an email

post-click metrics: Browsing, carting, and other activities on your site that take place after someone clicks through one of your emails

preference center: Webpage that displays a subscriber's email address and other details, such as profile information (zip code, etc.) and communication preferences (topics of interest, etc.), and allows them to make changes as well as unsubscribe

preheader text: HTML text positioned at the very top of an email's body content that is most often used to reinforce or extend the subject line; *also see* **snippet text**

preview pane: A window in some email clients that allows subscribers to view a smaller portion of an email than if the email were opened in its own window

preview text: *see* **snippet text**

primary message: The main message of an email, which is usually positioned at the top of the email and larger than other messages in the email

product grid: A multi-column and usually multi-row layout where each grid cell contains a product image and other information, such as product name, brand, and price

progressive profiling: Collecting additional demographic data and information about interests from subscribers by periodically asking them questions via email

quality assurance: Ensuring that email content is error-free and functions properly and that the intended subscribers receive that content at the intended time

reactivate: *see* ***reengage***

reactivation email: *see* ***reengagement email***

reading pane: *see* ***preview pane***

real list growth: A measure of the change in subscriber lifetime value of a list, this metric subtracts the value of subscribers lost over a period of time from the value of those gained during that period; *also see* ***absolute list growth*** *and* ***engaged list growth***

recovery module: A secondary content block usually positioned right before the footer that contains many links to different product categories, brands, or other areas of your website that is designed to appeal to subscribers who were uninterested in the other calls-to-action in the email

reengage: Getting a subscriber to open or click one of your emails after a long period of having not done so

reengagement email: A message sent to an individual subscriber in response to that person having not engaged with your emails or made a purchase in a long time in an effort to get them to engage and make a purchase again

relevance: How valuable a subscriber thinks your emails are—which is largely determined by how many emails you send, when they arrive, their content, and how they look and function within whichever email client is being used

rendering: How an email client translates an email's coding and displays the email

re-permission email: A message that asks a subscriber to reconfirm their subscription by clicking a link in the email in order to remain on your active mailing list

responsive email design: Advanced design techniques

that produce versions or renderings of an email that are optimized for particular screen resolutions or email clients

rich email content: Video consoles and other email content that subscribers can interact with without leaving their inbox

role-based email address: An email address that begins with *webmaster@*, *sales@*, *info@*, *press@*, or a similar function-based descriptor denoting that messages sent to this address are likely seen by or forwarded to more than one person

scalable email design: *see mobile-aware email design*

seasonality: Related to an upcoming or current season, holiday, or buying occasion

secondary message: The other message(s) in an email, usually following and smaller than the primary message

secondary navigation bar: Typically positioned right below your standard nav bar, this nav bar provides deeper navigation into one of your standard nav bar links, links to seasonal merchandise and content, or links that support the primary message or theme of the email

segmentation: Sending a particular message to only those subscribers who are likely to respond based on their geography, demographics, behavior, or other factors; or sending the same message to subscribers at different times based on their time zone or geography

sender name: The name that appears in the *from* line in an email client

sender reputation: A reflection of your trustworthiness as an email sender that is affected by spam complaint rates and other factors that internet service providers use to determine whether to deliver, junk, or block your email

shared IP address: An IP address from which multiple companies send email, with all of them contributing to the sender reputation of that address; *also see dedicated IP address*

share with your network (SWYN): Functionality that

allows subscribers to add content from your email to their social media timeline so their network of friends, family members, and other connections can see it

shopping cart abandonment email: A message sent to an individual subscriber in response to that person leaving one or more unpurchased items in their shopping cart

snippet text: A portion of the first text from inside the email that some email clients display after the subject line in the inbox, when highlighting a new email's arrival, or in other situations; *also see **preheader text***

social media bar: A row of social media icons that link to your brand's pages on those social media sites

social sign-in: Using the login information from a social network to sign in to a third-party website

spam: Any email that recipients consider unwanted or irrelevant—even if it's from brands they know and even if they gave the brand permission to email them

spam complaint: When an email recipient hits the Report Spam or Junk button, indicating to their ISP that the email was unwanted or irrelevant and that future emails from the sender are to be blocked

spamtrap: Whether they are long-abandoned, uncirculated, or contain a typo, these email addresses are used by ISPs and blacklisting organizations to identify spammers

split testing: *see **A/B testing***

static image: An image that doesn't change over time, unlike an animated gif

statistically significant: Having enough data from a test that the results are meaningful rather than simply the result of chance

still image: *see **static image***

subject line: The text that appears in the *subject* line in an email client

subject line quick link: A native inbox link positioned by the subject line that lets subscribers click through to the email's primary landing page without opening the email

subscriber: Someone who has consented to joining your email list

subscriber-level filtering: When an ISP junks and blocks all email sent by a brand to one of its email users; *also see **global filtering***

subscriber lifecycle: The various stages that a subscriber passes through from the time that they sign up until the time that they unsubscribe or otherwise cease receiving emails from a brand, including the stages of acquisition, onboarding, engagement, super-engagement, reengagement, and transition

subscriber lifetime value: The cumulative profit generated by a subscriber during their time on your list

subscriber replacement rate: The number of new subscribers a brand needs to add to its list over a period of time to replace those lost over that same period in order to maintain the size of its list

subscription activation email: *see **opt-in confirmation email***

super-engagement: Tactics that further engage subscribers who are already highly engaged

swipe file: A record of your top-performing emails, subject lines, calls-to-action, content blocks, landing pages, and other email elements that you return to for learnings and inspiration

system text: *see **HTML text***

tap: *see **click***

targeting: Sending the right message to the right subscriber at the right time

throttling: When an internet service provider slows the rate at which they deliver a sender's emails to their users

total weight: *see **loaded weight***

total clicks: The number of times the links or linked

images in an email were selected by subscribers, who then visited the associated landing page; a method of measuring opens that includes repeat clicks by an individual subscriber

total opens: The number of times the images of an email were loaded or rendered; a method of measuring opens that includes repeat opens by an individual subscriber

transactional email: A message sent to an individual subscriber in response to that person making a transaction, such as a purchase (e.g., order confirmation emails, shipping notification emails, etc.) or an administrative request (e.g., password reset email, email address change confirmation email, etc.)

triggered email: A message sent to an individual subscriber in response to an action taken by that person (e.g., cart abandoned) or because of the arrival of an event indicated by the subscriber (e.g., their birthday)

unique clicks: The number of subscribers who selected a link or linked image in an email at least once and visited the associated landing page; a method of measuring clicks that only counts the first click made by individual subscribers, ignoring any subsequent clicks

unique opens: The number of subscribers who loaded or rendered the images of an email at least once; a method of measuring opens that only counts the first open made by individual subscribers, ignoring any subsequent opens

unsubscribe: When a subscriber requests to be removed from a brand's email list

unsubscribe page: Webpage that is launched when subscribers click the unsubscribe link in your emails where subscribers complete the unsubscribe process

unsubscribe process: How subscribers remove themselves from your email list

video gif: A compressed, streaming animated gif capable of video-quality frame rates

webmail: An email client that's accessed solely online;

also see **app-based email**

weight: The file size of the HTML coding of an email; *also see* **loaded weight**

welcome email: A message automatically sent to a new subscriber just after they've opted in that welcomes them to your email program and seeks further engagement; *also see* **welcome email series**

welcome email series: Multiple emails automatically sent to a new subscriber over time that seek to maximize engagement

withhold study: When a brand doesn't send emails to a portion of their list for a period to measure what effect that lack of messaging has on that group's spending across all channels compared to subscribers who continued to receive emails during that period

win-back email: *see* **reengagement email**

Figures

Diagrams, Illustrations, and Charts